{Arabiolosis}

MAZRI'S **10** LAWS FOR CONVERTING FROM

A FEELING SPECIES TO A THINKING SPECIES

Nathen Mazri

Contents

All that is written here is based on true facts, narrated by Nathen Mazri. Names have been changed to protect the identity and privacy of the individuals concerned The matters publicized in this book should not be considered of legitimate public interest or general opinion; rather, they reflect the author's personal opinion based on experience.

Dedicated to my dear mother, great father, protective

brothers, lovely sister

and

my sole God.

{Arabiolosis} (n):

a form of suppression of that
particular culture

CHAPTER ONE

THE LOCK-UP

Mazri's Law #1

**Only in the darkest shadows
will the brightest ideas emerge.
Embrace the unordinary,
the uncommon, the unlikely
for an extraordinary life.**

I recall the time when I was ten years old, back in Montreal, standing beside my mother as she received a phone call from my dad. He was settling in the wealthy Kingdom of Saudi Arabia, where he had been offered an excellent opportunity as CEO of a large American IT company based in the capital city, Riyadh. He was telling us to prepare ourselves for a magic carpet ride to the Middle East, where we might stay forever. We were ecstatic. My mom did the chicken dance and we gave each other high fives, because we knew that our lifestyle would improve. Mom understood better than I that the money would not only be more plentiful, but it would also go farther toward buying the things we wanted, leading to happiness. I was content to simply go see my cousins, about whom I had heard so much—and also to see my grandmother, Noel Mazri, who had stolen my heart on the day I was born. The funny thing is that I had no idea what was waiting for me there. To this very day, I look back at that naïve little boy who was overexcited to hear life changing news.

That is where it all started . . . but I can't tell you everything yet.

I have turned my back on various joyful memories in Montreal. I have left out the girl who shared my first kiss, and to whom I never had the opportunity to say good-bye, with whom I shared a strong friendship between six-year-olds who could have grown up together—but didn't.

The most memorable picture instilled in my psyche is that of a full house, a family of seven members (my parents, brother, sister, two uncles, and me) all under one roof. In addition, there were the occasional visits of my long-lost big half-brother, Ally—given up at six years old by my mother to my grandparents, who at the age of 60 raised a little boy all over again as if they hadn't done enough raising five children of their own. It could have been a sad story; but it turned to a life of success that could be a memoir in itself. Ally is the true epitome of self-mastery, who has endured the loss of biological family, living twenty years in internal conflict, burying the answers of his true individuality and self-worth, which he was compelled to discover solo, becoming his own man at last, infused with self-rehabilitating thoughts and today serving as a life coach to my soul.

That said, Ally and I did not get along well when we were children, as there were unresolved and underlying emotions that kept growing stronger, fueling me with anger and animosity toward him and vice-versa. Why? Simple! We were both competing for that one mother's love!

Our house had always possessed an enthusiastic spirit. My uncle Eddie—the youngest of seven siblings—was adventurous and playful. He would wrestle me to the ground, wrapping his legs around my body; I would struggle to free myself until I ran out of breath, but he had no mercy. He claims it was fun. My brother and I would come down to Eddie's room in the basement every morning while he was still asleep and tickle his feet or make sounds. When he showed signs of waking up, we would rush upstairs—and, of course, come back down later as if we'd done nothing.

The image of my Montreal home during those years could be a fast-moving montage set to music; you would see one person leaving, another arriving, my mom cooking, and my dad entering the house with toys in his hands for the three of us.

One day my uncle Eddie bought us a PlayStation videogame set with a half-dozen games and full accessories, including special controllers for the car-racing and airplane games. My cousins had been flaunting their new PlayStation, reveling in the joy of what they owned. I think it was less shame at their behavior and more sympathy for our heartache and envy that compelled Uncle Eddie to be so generous.

In these memories, we abided with no trouble: these were simple, happy days—before I realized how dramatically and completely life can change.

Finally, the day for which we were waiting arrived. But our destination was not the Middle East, but the middle of nowhere. We had packed up more than twenty boxes along with our luggage, which we lined up outside randomly to be placed in the moving truck. It was hectic that day; the mood in our house was like we were waiting for a hurricane to make landfall. Being surrounded by friends and family empowers you. People empower other people. You feel important, confident, and free when you belong to a group of friends.

Trudeau Airport in Montreal was a river of tears—except for my grandpa. I had never seen him cry. He couldn't even bring himself to say, "Farewell, my daughter." Instead, he turned his back and walked like a man who has lost a fortune, staring at the floor. But my mother wouldn't leave without saying farewell; she followed him, calling out, dropped her bags and opened her arms wide. Finally, they embraced with a silent cry and rapid tears of sorrow.

My grandma hadn't even come to the airport; she had finished her goodbyes from home and then gone for a walk. So my family and I walked away down the terminal and never looked back at our hometown again. But I wish I had.

After thirteen hours of flying, the plane landed in Khobar, Saudi Arabia, and opened its doors. My brother, mother, and sister walked down the stairs before I did; I paused for a few seconds, feeling the hot breeze blowing in my face. I had never experienced tropical heat before. and I can still recall that mind-altering updraft as if it were yesterday. Then I descended the stairs, gazing at the exotic palm trees.

I proceeded across the tarmac into the airport. The numerous queues were crowded with people unlike any I had ever seen before—just different and eccentric. Beyond the passport-checking counter, I saw a woman in whose face was written a nature that was altruistic, benevolent, and loving. I stared at this grand woman with an uncertain feeling of recognition.

"Go ahead," I heard my mother say. "It's your grandmother!"

As soon as the words were spoken, I felt the urge to run and cuddle her for eternity; but we were still stuck in the passport queue. As soon as we were finished, I ran to her, running like Superman does when he wants to save lives. I gave myself over to my longing for my dear grandma. She gathered me in her arms and kissed me all over my face.

Seconds later, I saw my father coming toward us. He'd been away for almost two years, settling in Riyadh in order to prepare a life for us. After hugs and kisses, we found out that there was something wrong with my passport, and we would have to wait until it was resolved before we could leave. We waited for three hours in the airport, late at night. The place was nearly empty aside from us, with not even one clerk— okay, maybe one, but not many. How peculiar it was that from the very first step I made into this country, its dark shadows began to emerge at me—and only me.

The security officers were kind, though. They offered us *kabsa*, a famous Saudi dish of chicken on a bed of rice prepared with spices, which give the whole dish an golden yellow color. It is a traditionally eaten by hand, but we had chosen to eat with a nice silver spoon—our first meal in the Kingdom. By the time we finished eating, the commander had resolved the passport issue, and we were allowed to go.

After the airport, we hit the road to my cousins' house; we would stay with them for the next week, until our place was ready. Their home was a cement building. It was unlike anything I had been used to back in Montreal, defying my sense of what a house or an apartment should be. Even the way that sound reverberated in the building sounded strange.

When we entered, I heard screams of joy and welcome, which made me more anxious and excited. My aunt was standing on the stairs with open arms, hollering my name. She grabbed me and cuddled me, planting kisses here and there. Three more stairs up was my cousin Nina, the oldest girl of the Mazri family, face as pale as Jane Eyre's and completely innocent and free of peccadilloes. She grabbed me and squeezed me tightly.

When I walked to the door of their three-and-a-half-room apartment, I saw a girl standing there, looking like Juliet waiting for her Romeo. I felt as if I'd known her for years. This was Noel—the same name as my sister, both of them named for my paternal grandmother. I have never felt so powerful and loved as I did seeing the physical joy on their faces, beaming at me.

More intense salutations awaited me, as we are part of a substantial family. As the greetings went on, I found myself looking for someone—the old man I had seen in a photograph back in our home in Montreal. In the picture, he was standing up straight, dressed in a suit, regarding the camera with a furrowed face—stringent and serious, yet kind. As I gazed to my right, the same old man was sitting on the sofa: my grandpa. He started laughing as soon as he saw me, as if I were a long-lost son rescued from oblivion.

Over the next week I got used to the family and quickly became closer to my cousins. Soon it was time for my family, grandparents, and me to take the four-hour road trip to the middle of the desert to Riyadh—the capital city of Saudi Arabia, our future home, where it all happened! Here we would live with my grandparents until our own house was ready.

Saudi Arabia is a country built on desert, with a hot, dry climate; temperatures regularly reach 45 degrees Celsius (113 degrees Fahrenheit)—about the same temperature as the seventh floor of Hell. When we arrived in Riyadh, it seemed as if immense black gates had slammed shut, locking behind us and wrapped in chains, with the keys thrown into quicksand so as never to be found again—at least not soon enough.

One evening, my Uncle Robert came to pick us up from grandma's place. I sat in the front passenger seat of his fancy car at the front passenger seat, gazing out the window at the buildings. The houses were made completely of cement, with outer walls surrounding each one of them like a fortification. It was so unlike Canada, where neighborhoods look and feel open. Profound darkness lay all around; the looming shadows seemed like a place where devils might lurk.

As we reached his house, making our entrance, Uncle Robert told us to keep quiet and stay in the outer hallway; he would enter first to keep the surprise from his family, who had no idea that we had arrived. Indeed, it had been four years since we had seen one another.

After he made his entrance and closed the hall door, we paused a moment before entering furtively. Coming into the living room, we saw my Aunt Victoria and cousins (in order of age) Alanis, Paris, Lee, and Hilary. They jumped from their seats, screaming with joy. We embraced, laughed, and shed some happy tears. The sense of love and welcome was palpable. Aunt Victoria, Alanis, and Paris would soon become an inspiration to me during my journey—and my battle with what was waiting to eat me alive.

In the days to come, we make more visits and meet still more cousins, including those on our father's side, who would become our closest new friends. What can I say? We are a large clan!

After four months of staying with my grandma, my dad finally found us a place of our own. It was located in a compound that consisted of six condos with one big swimming pool and a long front yard. The whole complex was surrounded by a big wall; this kind of construction is quite common in the Kingdom, and is intended to secure the women from being disclosed to manly eyes. Men are deprived of the sight of a woman, as she is compelled to wear a long black robes called an *abaya*. If she fails to veil herself, there may be serious consequences; religious police officers may take her to jail, or she may come into conflict with her guardian—that is, her husband or father. Because men are institutionally deprived of contact with the opposite gender, if a woman reveals herself physically it will definitely lead to harassment, which can range from playful flirtation to vicious abuse. And so the custom of the Kingdom mandates these grand residential walls, which serve to extend privacy and security in case a woman would like to stand outside of her house, take a swim, or even throw out the garbage.

During our first week in our big new condo, we slept on mattresses on the floor and with air conditioners running in every room. I would wake up with the sun brightly illuminating the entire house and with the mechanical noise of the air conditioners humming in my ears.

Our moving truck finally arrived in Riyadh from Canada on October 28—my brother Moe's birthday. My family and I were very cheerful that day, eager to open the boxes and see our belongings. In the condos beneath our new home were neighbors with whom we would soon become acquainted.

This was my first experience of such an environment. It seemed very peculiar in a structural and atmospheric way; as a ten-year-old newcomer, I didn't think very highly of Saudi

Arabia compared to Canada, but there was still much more for me to see. At that particular time, the gates of Hell were utterly closed, leading to no escape and the rise of the demons punctually planning and moving at a fast pace for torment.

* * *

I had always wanted a baby brother or sister in the house, someone I would cuddle while small and eventually romp with. I used to pray every day for one. I would tell my mom that I wanted to have a baby sibling, and she would always reply, "Three is enough! Shut up."

One day not long after our move, she felt pain in her stomach and went to the doctor. It turned out to be a miracle for me—and darkness for her: she was unexpectedly pregnant.

As the unbelievable news spread, friends and family were laughing with joy, telling her this baby was bound to be on this Earth. My mother, though, seemed gloomy at times. My grandma kept telling her, "Never question God's will. If he wants it in this world, it is going to come, no matter what."

Sometimes my mom would stay up all night, moaning in pain and holding her stomach for what seemed like hours. I felt responsible. Was this how God had answered my prayers?

During my mother's pregnancy, I felt what a mother has to go through to get me and my siblings, understanding that she had endured this four times in years past. Looking back, I realized my mother had carried a worried face since the very

11

day we had arrived in Riyadh. Sometimes I would feel so upset over the sorrows she bore that I would shed silent tears in sympathy.

Our condo was really too small for us. My parents hated that it had a single spacious room with no partition for a sitting room and a salon. We had to put both in one room—a salon on the right side and the living room on the left. Plus, we had lots of problems from the neighbors next to us; they were newlyweds, and they didn't want to put up with so many noisy children. Sometimes when we were outside playing or swimming with our cousins, the husband or the wife would come out, yelling at us to be quiet.

One day while my mom was pregnant with her last, unexpected baby, she decided she'd had enough. She knocked on this neighbor's door; as soon as the lady opened it, my mom screamed at her with an anger level reaching the top of the thermometer. The lady stood there without a word. After a few minutes of this, our neighbor Ariel, came and led my mom back to the house, saying that so much screaming would be bad for the baby. The neighbor lady closed the door and we never heard from her again. Mom was always aggressive in defense of her children; if anything ever came in the way of her youngsters, the lioness would roar, step up, and maybe rip its guts out.

The summer of the millennium year was a climax of sorts,

bringing changes both for the worse and the better. My cousins who lived in the same building as my grandma were moving to Lebanon. It was extremely hard on my grandma, as she had never left them for one second since the day my aunt was born. She cried for two days and nights. On the night of their departure, the whole family came to our house, gathering around my grandma who sat on the sofa sobbing inconsolably. My mother tried to reassure her that she hadn't lost her daughter; after all. Libya was only two hours away by plane.

That summer, we returned to Montreal for a long stay, with Dad staying behind in Saudi Arabia. The baby was due in mid-September, and my parents had decided that he should be born in Canada. While we were away, my dad called with big news. At last, he had found us a house of our own—a big single-family villa with four bedrooms and five bathrooms, exactly as my mother wanted. There would be no trouble with neighbors, since there were privacy walls surrounding the house on a par with the Great Wall of China. It was exactly the kind of house we had always wanted. Better still, it stood directly across the street from the home of our German cousins. My father assured us that all our belongings would be moved in by the time we returned to the Kingdom.

On September 15, 2000, at 11:59 AM, my mother gave birth to my brother Eddie at St. Mary's Hospital. My aunt Victoria stayed with her throughout the whole ordeal, not

13

leaving her side for days. When I saw this baby soul for the first time in the hospital, I felt something inexplicable.

My heart fluttered at each step I took toward Eddie. Staring at him in his crib, I said to myself: *I will spoil you so badly, never yell at you I will make sure you never fall and that you have everything you want.* I wanted to be the big brother and treat him right.

Unfortunately, time has made me invisible along the way, and I have not been the best big brother someone could ask for.

After four months in Canada, it was finally time to head back to our new house and life with a new human being in tow. When we got to Riyadh, my dad picked us up from the airport in our new chauffeured car. After hugging and kissing us older children, he turned his attention to baby Eddie in his stroller. He stared silently for several seconds, then teasingly said to mom, "He has nothing to do with me. Are you sure he is mine?"

"He has the looks from my side of the family," retorted my mother. "It's my turn now."

As he carried Eddie, my dad had a smile up to his ears; he was overflowing with awe. He could not believe what he was seeing in front of him. You could see him content with utter pride.

Soon we were on our way to our new house. As we took a

left turn to enter the street, my mom recognized the place. "Oh my Go-o-od, kids," she cried with excitement. "Your dad and I used to pass by this street when we first came to this country. We used to wish we could live in one of these villas. But they were so expensive then!"

Stepping into the house, with the driver behind me carrying our luggage, I felt satisfied as well as self-important. I gave myself a tour in the house, anxious to see my new room. When I came back downstairs, my parents told me we were leaving again immediately to visit our grandparents, who wanted to see us—especially baby Eddie. I was keen to see my grandparents, too, and especially all of my cousins.

As soon as my grandpa opened the door, we could hear the loud greetings and excitement. After a lot of cuddles, they all moved in to see the new member of the family, the one I liked to call the Millennium Baby. Everyone wanted a piece of him, waiting in turn to carry him, and all commenting on how he took after my mother's side, the Sahabi family. They were stunned by his beauty, especially his rainbow eyes; their color seemed to change with the color of his shirt.

My grandma and I share a very special bond. I have always been known as her favorite. I am more than simply a grandson; rather, we are more like school friends who have grown up together. We joke, laugh, gossip, shop together, go to dinner, read together, and lean on each other. I loved to sleep over at her house on the weekends, as I had nowhere to go and no real best friend to talk to. She liked the days we spent together. She liked the company, and grandpa was glad to have someone in the house. I think we all filled some void in the other. When grandma visited us, she would ask me if I wanted to come back with her for a sleepover, and the two of us would concoct a persuasive plea that would convince my dad to concede. Whenever I came over, she would always ensure that I got five-star service during my stay.

She is a gossip girl, but with a spiritual side, and in some ways the traditional grandmother, left lonely as her children move on with their own lives. She always says that I am *her* child, conceived late in her years, and laughs loudly. *I* would never leave her behind. Anyway, why should I leave, when it took me years to get here?

My first four years in Saudi Arabia were fascinating; everything was different and alien to my eyes. I had so much to learn about the country's nature, physical structure, and environment—even about my own extended family. It was an entirely new life where I had no worries—well, perhaps some. But they weighed very little as yet. I was young, and ready for adventure. Everything was good in this place, so far. I was living comfortably, my dreams weren't very definite, and the word "misery" was as yet hard for me to spell.

This would change soon enough, as there is always an

opportunity in every difficulty.

What is the theme of Chapter 1?

Your family and friends define your "chatterbox"—the voice in your subconscious that you hear throughout your childhood and which shapes your personality, attitude, beliefs, and even destiny. You will identify these voices as either wrong or right as you grow up, and self-correct to develop your *true* identity and passion. Do not give in to those inner voices just yet.

Be self-aware!

CHAPTER TWO

CULTURE CLASH

Mazri's Law #2

You can never take away people's perception of you, and other people can never take away your self-esteem; but with your self-esteem, you can alter other people's perceptions— and build a country.

I will never forget what my best friend told me back in the sixth grade. He saw me sitting alone on a bench in the playground waiting for the morning bell, came up to me, and said, "It doesn't suit you to be alone." If he only knew how alone I truly was!

So far, this new world was more like the underworld. I thought it would be an adventure to move to a place I could explore, to learns about new people and a new atmosphere. However, sometimes a place is just not right for you, and no one will really understand that fact. You don't feel genuinely yourself because you can't be yourself when you live where you don't belong. Even though you try to socialize, you just can't do it with this kind of crowd; you can't adopt their breezy state of mind. It is an unhealthy situation. It is people that make life interesting, make you forget your worries, and fill your existence with delight. So imagine there are no *Homo sapiens* in your life. What will be your next play?

And that's just the beginning of my move to this miserable place and how it left me feeling deprived.

The underworld has a dry atmosphere, and it is boiling, with temperatures regularly topping 100 degrees Fahrenheit (38 Celsius). There are hardly any green lawns or pleasing scenery—nothing compared to what my eyes are used to. No sea or crystal beach. Oh, but wait! There is a lake called Leila in Dammam! Unfortunately, it has evaporated due to global warming. Oh, well!

A demon had tempted me to move to the underworld by taking advantage of my deep love for my family circle. Then it cleared the battlefield, vanquishing relatives and friends back to their homelands. All of them had lived here all their lives—yet when I came along, smelling of the desert, they suddenly disappeared, one family after another, leaving me alone and occupied.

The demon's first assault took the form of an extreme culture clash, which left me perturbed on a daily basis. I began experiencing these aliens in disguises the moment I entered high school. I was young for my class, having skipped the eighth grade. I worked hard to make this leap; I wanted to finish school as quickly as I could so I could leave the Kingdom and go to university back in Canada. I was fighting and bleeding to save that one more year.

In my experience, teenagers and young adults are critical and judgmental in attitude, while lacking in real ethics or morals. I am speaking of young men, as all schools are divided by gender. Mixing of genders anywhere in Saudi Arabia is prohibited by law. I have even seen McDonald's separated in two—one section for families and another for men only! There are also major malls made only for women to enter—except for the male mutaween who wander about telling people what to do in their daily lives. The mutaweens' responsibility in Saudi Arabia is to enforce *Sharia*, or Islamic law—at least, the version of Sharia as defined by the government. The 3,500 mutaween employed by the Commission for the Promotion of Virtue and the Prevention of Vice (CPVPV), along with thousands of volunteers, are often accompanied by a police escort; they roam the streets, major malls, restaurants, department stores, and even IKEA, and wield the power to arrest unrelated males and females caught socializing, or anyone engaged in homosexual behavior or prostitution. They enforce Islamic dress codes and force stores to close during the five-times daily prayers. They enforce Muslim dietary laws prohibiting the consumption or sale of alcoholic beverages and pork, and seize banned consumer products and media regarded as un-Islamic, such as CDs or DVDs of various Western musical groups, television shows, and films. Additionally, they actively prevent the practice of other religions within Saudi Arabia, where they are banned.

The mutaween have been criticized for the use of flogging to punish violators, and for banning Valentine's Day gifts. Perhaps the most serious scandal attributed to them occurred on March 11, 2002, when they prevented schoolgirls from escaping a burning school in Mecca, because the girls were not wearing headscarves and *abayas* and were not accompanied by a male guardian. Fifteen girls died and fifty were injured as a result. Widespread public criticism followed, both internationally and within Saudi Arabia.

I always felt uncomfortable when surrounded by *Them*, young adults with a cynical and chastising state of mind. They are narrow-minded, operating solely on the basis of the stereotypes that fill the air like oxygen here. And they have appointed themselves to police the boundaries between masculinity and femininity.

For instance, it is very important to know how and what to say in public spaces. Words with strong vowel sounds, delivered in a soft tone, mark the speaker as feminine and unmanly. The more points you rack up in the category of femininity, the closer you are to automatically being perceived and stereotyped as homosexual. Keep your voice harsh and project a thuggish attitude, the more points you accumulate for being masculine; and the more masculine you are, the more you'll be respected and feared.

Let's consider the division based on the nature of pairs of words like "Hi" and "Wassup," "gang" and "group," and "bush" and "flower." The words "Wassup," "gang," and "bush" are considered more masculine words than "Hi," "group," and "flower."

Once, I was on the basketball court talking to a couple of guys and I used the phrase "group of friends." One of the guys focused on the word "group," out of all of the thousand words I had said.

He giggled for a while, then said, "A *gang*, not a *group*, man. Yo, check out what he said."

The same rule holds for colors in clothing; anything light in color (e.g., a shirt) is not accepted; rather, something dark would be more normal and usual. Paying attention to fashion in general creates a conflict with regard to gender distinction. A *GQ* man—that is, someone dressed according to the trend—raises heads and turns eyes. If he's walking down the sidewalk to the market or to school, the sight of a well-dressed man will draw stares. Perhaps there's some attraction there. Why are they looking in the first place? There has to be something that deeply appeals to them—especially if he dyes his hair, which makes him a blatant target.

Unveil What Lies Beneath the Desert

Saudi Arabia is, of course, the Number One oil exporter in the world. However, it also holds a second title: most sexually repressed country in the world, after the Philippines. In a country where even straight sex is repressed, gay sex is anathema. But the level of taboo seems to be correlated with the level of social interest. In Saudi Arabia, religious extremists rule over everyone—but gay life flourishes in a closed society where men and women are separated in every way, which only exacerbates the homosexual urges some people feel beginning at puberty. From the time they start school, men only have access to other men, with urges starting in the sixth grade. Sexual activities in same-gender schools can range from simply showing each other one's penis to kissing and touching each other inappropriately.

The irony is that regardless of Islamic law's prohibition of homosexuality, the social taboos against drinking, clubbing, or mixing with an unrelated person of the opposite gender—all of which are enforced by the mutaween—make it almost easier to be gay than straight here. You can't even be spotted with a girlfriend, or else you will have to endure the forty lashes on your back and an undetermined period of time in prison before being deported. Mutaween are most likely to punish men who are conspicuously feminine. Filipino guest workers, in particular, seem to be very vulnerable.

Gay men live a private life and can seldom be accused of living a deviant lifestyle unless a *mutawaa* intrudes into his privacy at home to see who shares his bed, which is ridiculously implausible.

Homosexual men often gather in Starbucks, Fitness First or other commercial restaurants and cafés. These are among their secret underground places to hang out and pick up men. In the virtual world, you will need to download an anchor-free software that interrupts the IP address, giving you access to all the sites blocked by the government. Otherwise, trying to access a gay hookup site will give you a message in bold type: "Sorry, the requested page is unavailable. If you believe the requested page should not be blocked, please click here." And you really don't want to click here.

Single gay men are everywhere; you just need to have a good gaydar and it's a date! Arabs love white and fair-skinned men with light hair. You will never find my Canadian cousin, Brian, with his soft blond hair, wandering the streets of Riyadh unless he desires to get raped by the sexually suppressed predators. The Saudis will seduce you wherever you are! Lebanese men are also highly favored by those in the neighboring countries, who describe them as the most beautiful men of the Middle East.

The segregation of the sexes allows for gay desire among women, too. Although women have fewer venues to gather publicly without male supervision, lesbians find ways to connect—even on the grounds of all-girl high schools. A few years ago, a newspaper based in Jeddah ran a story about girls having sex in bathrooms.

According to the Saudi perspective, little or no stigma is attached to playing the dominant role (or the "top") during sexual intercourse. The ignominy and disgrace lies in being the recipient during sex. A man that has intercourse with another man is not "gay" unless he is the bottom. The top man may be in denial, but does not consider himself a homosexual but rather as a "real man," free of stigma and shame. The sense of disgrace around here lies in the distinction between taking pleasure and being used for pleasure.

Homosexual men with white-collar jobs fly out of the country from time to time, sometimes spending weekends in neighboring countries with more liberty, in order to relieve their sexual desires. The feeling is, "If sex does not come to me, then I have the means to go to it!"

Confusion of faith lies in the hearts of Muslims, causing an identity crisis. They comprehend that gay activity is sinful under Islamic law, and one who practices it will be heavily punished by God on Judgment Day. However, they also believe that God is merciful and forgiving if you're pure at heart, repent, and obey God by praying five times a day, fasting during Ramadan, and giving *zakat,* or annual donations to an accredited Islamic charitable organization.

For centuries, the western LGBT community has devoted hard work and dedication to ensuring the right to living a peaceful gay lifestyle and expressing pride in one's sexual orientation, seeking support and acceptance around the world through gay pride events and parades. But don't the holy books, the Bible and the Quran alike, say "Thou shalt not lie with mankind, as with womankind: it is an abomination" (Leviticus 18:22)? Is it religion vs. modernism now?

Some say our sexual orientation is set from birth, and others say it arises from sinful temptation. Scientists have never had a definite answer; but homosexuality has entered the public sphere as a subject worthy of discourse, rather than something to be feared and ignored. Scientists are thus able to invest time and money into research yielding headlines such as "Biology is Behind Homosexuality in Sheep, Study Confirms" (*Health and Medicine Week* issue 422, 2004).

In the Middle East, though, the attitude is "Don't ask, don't tell"— and government officials know it. It is natural for young people to act on their early feelings of sexual arousal at any time. And because unmarried men and women are not allowed together in public, they will explore their sexual urges with the only people of the opposite gender whose company is permitted them—that is, their cousins—or simply try to suppress their feelings. Watch the anxiety and stress level hit the ceiling!

Could suppression, lack of communication and companionship from females, genetics, rebellious attitude, father issues, and lack of masculine influence during childhood shape your sexuality forever?

Not one day passed by without hearing the word "gay" used as a statement of ridicule. I believe such behavior in young men and boys is largely due to their own possible attraction to the same gender, and their need to deny it. Therefore, to hide their true identity, they act thuggish on the outside, as it appears more manly and straight.

Every day as I left for school, I would be gripped with the fear that I'd have to endure some verbal abuse, because I am a guy who supports everything that they are against. I seem to be a threat of some kind, and that keeps them on my back day after day.

Further down the line, in high school, the culture kept clashing against my persona, causing insecurity. I became plagued by self-doubt; every single criticism and negative remark went into my memory box in the corner of my mind. I felt that I was simply *wrong*, that everything about me was wrong!

But whatever I felt around these people, I would still leave for school being myself, keeping my personal style and vibrant personality. Nevertheless, deep down inside, I was not totally at ease with myself. There were constant critical voices in my head, and never-ending worries: *What if I get picked on because of this shirt? What if they all hate my shoes, or the way I will recite a poem in class after recess?* The refrain *What if?* ran through my head daily, now that I knew how critical the culture of this country was. And yet I wanted to belong. I would battle myself every day, asking: *Why I can't blend in? Why can't I be part of these people? Why can't I have normal friends?*

As I progressed through high school, I came to understand the actions of my peers, and the state of mind that drove them. These adolescents seemed to have no values or ethics of their own, and only strove to attain an ideal of western "cool"—an ideal they constructed from their (mis)understanding of American media. They emulate western culture as they see it, but they are completely blind to the reality of American culture, which is all about freedom and acceptance—of yourself and others. Due to the lack of personal agency and self-esteem, coupled with an abundance of ego, the society tends to be prejudiced, disparaging, and disapproving of others. And so the youth enforce the very boundaries that constrain them, following the path laid down for them by the country's civilization and their parents—at the expense of expressing who they really are and what they really want to do in life. They are very concerned with acting like men; as a consequence, they behave like troubled children.

To this day, I do not understand what makes a "true man" in this culture. Is a man always egotistical and always on the defensive? Does a man always have to do what his dad says? If he does not, is he no longer a man? Does a man have to wear ill-fitting clothes? Must a man always have a rough tone of voice? Does being a man mean not grooming yourself and paying a hefty price for looking immaculate? Does being a man mean fighting in the street? Does a man have to constantly chastise other men?

If that is the man they want me to be, then I will be happy to be called a girl. Someone call Dr. Phil, ASAP!

I felt uncomfortable and withdrawn with every moment of proximity to them—a sense of no belonging. So much for satisfying Maslow's hierarchy of needs! What's funny is that they are all homogenous in mentality and behavior. It is as if the whole country is infected with the same virus. It is epidemic. I knew that I was different and couldn't blend in easily; but the question at the front of my mind was *Why?* Was it me, or was it them?

My lack of self-confidence seemed to hobble my body, freezing me with an inability to be myself until I hardly knew what to say or do in any moment. I worried about how people perceived me—whether they liked me or not—and would become preoccupied with thousands of thoughts: *What did so-and-so say about me, and why? How and why they are looking at me?*

Every day at 3:30 PM, our driver would pick me up from school. At home, I would go upstairs, give my dirty clothes to the housekeeper, put on my pajamas, and come back downstairs to the kitchen where my mom would be cooking lunch. I'd sit there and wait till she asked me how my day had gone, or try to steer the conversation toward the main subject: *Them,* the people with a jaundiced eye. I longed to speak of my feelings, and the insecurity that paralyzed me. Finally, I'd start to tell her of some disturbing occurrences at school, and how I responded.

She would listen sympathetically, but at first her guidance amounted to, "Son, you think too much. And if all you do is think, you will never live your life."

Even as it became clear that the abuse and ostracism I suffered were not all in my mind, she advised me to adjust my attitude. "Nathen, my son, you should walk with your head high and your back straight. Why should you care what others say or think?" Her voice grew more aggressive "And by the way, who are they in the first place?"

I fell silent. It was some comfort to think that the boys who tormented me wore invisible tags stamped "Loser." It is a reassuring thought. I had sunk so deep into the culture that it had taken a toll on me, making me blind to the outside world. My mom opened my eyes, allowing me to look at the bigger picture—funny, considering it was I who had come from the outside world. Another scheme of the devil!

Still, I was in need of guidance. I became open to advice or uplifting words from anyone willing to give them. I was ready to listen.

At least I felt less like an outcast with my dear cousins and friends, Alanis and Paris. They were the only power girls to whom I could truly relate in this Kingdom of Saudi Arabia. We would have long conversations about the country's eccentric mentality, behavior, and attitudes. Talking with them, I felt less lonely and more self-righteous. There was nothing wrong with *me*. They made me feel that I was right and the others—the closed-minded people—were wrong. The three of us understood each other. Life is about belonging to a like-minded group. Isn't that the base of the pyramid of social needs in Maslow's hierarchy?

I idolized my cousins, especially Alanis, who was bold in character and indifferent to people's opinions of her. She was a petite beauty with her brown hair against her blue eyes and unique features, an exotic flower blooming in this arid place, with her own sense of style—she would later become a fashion designer—and a laughing spirit, always ready to ridicule the foolishness around us. She had endured dark circumstances of her own; her character was formed in the culture clash of her own formative years. But he had survived on hope and faith in God, knowing that everything would be OK in the end. I related to her grand personality and attitude because I understood where she was coming from. This placed her on my team. Every time I felt down or driven to madness, approaching the aliens from outer space, I would think of her as a check against my insecurities.

Her sister Paris looked better than the real Paris. She carried her height and her long, silky blonde hair with a model's posture. But her looks belied a shrewdness you could see in her green eyes under her Chanel eyeglasses, which she wore when reading novels or biology textbooks. You never knew what would trigger her unpredictable sense of humor and cause her to flash a smile as deliciously white as a scoop of vanilla ice cream.

Even now, years after leaving Saudi Arabia, I still return to visit my favorite cousins and my Aunt Victoria. They are very lively, comical, fun and selfless. They are always up-to-date in styles and fashions. Victoria remains young at heart, with a lively mind; she is a woman of elegance and style who is talkative and sociable. She can be exceedingly critical sometimes, but it's always for your own benefit. I get along so smoothly with the three of them. They keep me intact and take me to a better world, one of acceptance and vitality—as it should be.

But even the love and support of these wonderful women could only help me so much. I felt ground down by the extreme monotony I experienced in this country of oppression. Not only are men deprived of women by authority, there is no freedom of any kind. There are municipal police in the capital who literally roam the streets telling people how to live—especially women. One day at a mall restricted for single men—rather, family only—I saw a woman on the floor screaming, held down by three cops, as a religious municipal officer, wearing a long brown cape seized her purse to search it. He tugged on the strap and she would spin around the floor in circles.

Usually, Muslims pray five times a day; therefore, all businesses, retailers, and centers are obliged by Saudi labor law to close during prayer times to allow the employees to go and pray. As if they do! The religious municipal officers disperse all over the area, ensuring every single business is closed down. If they find out that a store is still in operation, they will issue a first warning; the next time, they will shut it down entirely. They will even follow customers in the shopping malls, shouting, "Go pray this instant!" Not that they pray themselves; they're too busy bossing everyone around. Hypocrites!

Other than coercing people to pray, the mutaween act as the fashion police. But it's not like on *Entertainment Tonight*—if they don't like how you're dressed or groomed, the mutaween can make things very bad for you.

Sometimes, teenagers would come up against these officers. My cousin Bryan was one such victim. One Thursday night, he and his friends were pulled in off Tahleyah Street. Bryan's long blond hair, styled like Brad Pitt's, marked him as a target. The mutaween held him in the car. One took Bryan's mobile phone and scrolled through its features; finding some sexy cartoons, the officer laughed and shared the pictures with his partners, enjoying the sexual content. They went through Bryan's messages, demanding that he translate one short message in English into Arabic.

Things got worse for Bryan; eventually the mutaween forcibly shaved his head. His offense, in their view, was emulating a girl; a man should have his hair short.

And whenever loud music was heard from outside a house, you could expect a visit from the mutaween. Of course, they might let you off if you asked them to join the party, especially if there were lots of girls present. What a great way to show the pure religion of Islam!

During Ramadan, don't expect to satisfy even the most the basic bodily needs. All restaurants and markets are closed down until sunset. According to Saudi labor laws, no one is permitted to drink or eat in the office—not even foreign guest workers. If you found doing so by the mutaween, they will come and deport you at once. The same goes for drinking water in public.

It is respectable, faithful, and dignified to believe and abide by a particular religion and belief; but it is not necessary to take extreme measures against non-Muslims or non-practicing Muslims, or to enforce a set of restrictive practices, even to the point of depriving people of the basic necessities of life. Saudi Arabia should encourage us to embrace, comprehend, and love Islam with an open mind. But this overzealous aggression causes the world to think badly of our religion. Does the Islamic faith really demand such extreme measures? Perhaps not . . . but who am I to say?

It is extremists like the mutaween who make our fair religion seem so unbearable. Muslims themselves have portrayed a distorted image to the world about the religion. Their exaggerated behavior, indecorous actions, and threatening attitude has overshadowed what Islam is really about, and has caused hatred and misunderstanding around the world. And all because of one country's idiosyncratic interpretation of the faith. Unfortunate!

These restrictions on personal behavior make it nearly impossible for a person to simply be himself. You must take precautions on what to wear in public and how to wear it, as your outward appearance can make you a target. You have to consider the color, the cut, and the style of your clothes. I have always liked to be fashionable and on top of the trends, like any normal young man in the outside world. It is ridiculous how much negative attention this garnered, how I was stereotyped as a homosexual or as Americanized. When I would wear a stylish Zara shirt and a funky belt I brought back from Canada, my own father would say, "Don't go out like this! Take off the belt and change your shirt." But I was obstinate. I wore what I wanted, with absolute disregard for the culture's reaction; it seemed absurd to me that anyone should be bothered.

But my father *was* bothered. Sometimes I would remain housebound just so I wouldn't have to confront him. I felt uncomfortable with myself, uncomfortable around my own dad, because the culture we lived in deprived us of the value of acceptance.

Of course, the major reason that I would stay home and experience monotony is that there were no places to enjoy myself—nowhere to go at all for social purposes. There were no social establishments, no cinemas, nightclubs, or pubs; all were forbidden. If you wanted to dance, you did it in the shower; if you wanted to socialize, you talked to the walls. The hippest place perhaps to go was Starbucks.

The boredom was inescapable, with no diversion. All the "new release" movies were about two years old; if you wanted anything more recent ones, you had to find pirated copies on the black market—usually recorded in cinemas with smuggled camcorders. The hands of the censors touched even these. While watching a pirated movie you might notice a man getting up from his theatre seat semi-nude after screwing his wife (I know that because I saw it in Canada), but the on-screen action would have adulterous content or even kissing scenes excised. When I was watching a black-market version of *Titanic*, the scene where Leonardo DiCaprio and Kate Winslet have their moment in the car was not shown at all. It was as if this scene never existed—and the next thing you knew, the ship was sinking. How? Why? What happened? If you wanted to find out, you had to travel to the outside world and you'll know. For now, there is nowhere to go!

In Saudi Arabia, even the atmosphere isn't a pleasant one. There's nothing that could motivate you to leave your house to take a walk and get a breath of fresh air. Instead, it is a dry desert and an arid culture that simply dries up your life. And so the demon tormenting me had me exactly where he wanted me—stuck at home, isolated, with nothing to look forward to but one hardship after the other.

I began to live a very dull and routine life. Every avenue for change, even for small changes, was cut off, which widened my wound. Each dawn brought another tasteless and nail-biting day where I was compelled to face the culture clash as I left for school. Another day for me to endure their intolerance. I hardly ever heard words of motivation: no "Good job, man," or "You are good at that," or even "Nice shoes."

Such positive statements would never be spoken in this country, where criticism has become an unhealthy lifestyle!

After school it was back home for a family lunch. I would hope for it to go well; more and more often, my father came to the table in a grouchy mood. With nothing else to do, I took long naps in the afternoon and watched long hours of TV; for a diversion, I might check my email and surf the internet with low-speed dial-up, and maybe do some homework.

When the weekends came—which in Saudi Arabia means Thursdays and Fridays—it was literally "The End." These were the days where Mother Boredom took full control. There were family gatherings either at our place, Uncle Eddie's, or Uncle Moe's house—lunch, dinner, or just coffee—but it usually turned out the same way; my father and uncles would play chess for senseless hours, while their wives and kids (myself included) sat in the living room listlessly marking time. If you passed by, you might believe we were all sculptures stolen from a National Museum gallery.

When we first came to Saudi Arabia, before my Uncle Morris and Aunt Miriam moved away, the family used to make plans for the weekends. We would take outings to the desert, roving parties consisting of more than twenty family members and friends. But the event planners left the country one by one, and the stay-at-homes were left with no sense of adventure, doing the same old things all the time. Perhaps it was the only life they knew!

The fact that these dull gatherings were the only opportunity for leisure in my empty life spurred me to resent my own family for their way of living. My older relatives—father, uncles, grandma, even (in spite of his taciturn nature) grandpa—would all provoke me into feeling such negative feelings because of how they mandated this static social life.

One Thursday, the Mazri family were gathered at our house. We were all sitting in the living room—except, of course, for my dad and his brothers.

It was my birthday—March 27, 2002. I was not expecting any special treatment, as my family barely observes birthdays. And to tell the truth, I had started to lose interest in them. I always used to look forward to that day, as I desperately wanted to reach the age of eighteen; I thought at that age I would become independent and look like a jock. (Perhaps I was watching too much western TV.)

But in my teenage years, birthdays just made me sad. I looked at myself and my life and felt I had not accomplished as much as I'd expected. Perhaps my ambition was getting me down.

I kept on wandering aimlessly through the house; I felt angry at being trapped inside, and was desperately in need of someone to complain to. Returning to the living room, I rejoined the UN of the Mazris, sitting down beside my mom.

My aunt said, "You look bored."

Then my grandpa unexpectedly burst out, "You are *always* bored! What do you want? For my son to send you away alone to Canada?" He made a face of disgust. "You are such a disgrace to your country, wanting to leave so badly. Look at your brother—why is he not complaining, eh?"

I tried to defend myself, but my mom had also joined the argument; in the end, I said something rude and stormed off to my room.

I was that my father would be notified; surely he must hear me pacing back and forth in my room. The family disapproved of the very things that caused me trouble with my peers—my fashion, my ambitions, my flashy personality—and they thought I was mentally troubled.

My dad and I had a weak bond, as I had to put up with his dreary spirit at home and live according to his lifestyle. We didn't converse often. He didn't seem to recognize my interests. I wanted to broaden my horizons in life, satisfy my desires and curiosity. I tried to express this to him, but unfortunately he would give me less than constructive feedback—and nothing at all to feed my teenage intellect. We had no father-and-son activities we could plan or enjoy together. Our routines together were dull. There was no sense of enthusiasm in our relationship. When I pictured my father in my head, I saw a man with pessimistic face, saying "No" to everything.

It was bad enough to be chastised at school, but then to have to come home to an atmosphere of pressure, criticism, verbal abuse, mockery, or sarcasm from a father—it was too much. My dad is a very good person, generous and overprotective of his kids. "His love for his children is greater than his love for his wife," my mom would say. But he could not give me the kind of love I needed to ease my pain.

I lived with constant stress. Sometimes I would leave the living room as soon as my dad came in. It was almost involuntary; whenever I felt his presence, my body would sweep away unplanned. It was a reflex born from a negative cause—a lack of empathy from both parties, I would say. Nothing has an effect without a cause.

At that time, I was too weak to talk back and feared his anger. He made it hard on me to get closer to him, as if he were exercising the law of withdrawal. We were both obstinate, and would wait for the other to make the first move. Perhaps our bond was strained because I blamed him for my misery—for making us live in the middle of the desert. Shouldn't I have had a choice in that? Doesn't a normal family talk about such a life-changing occurrence?

That was my perspective, but again there was a culture clash—this one with my own father, over the nature of a father's authority. He is the dad; he is the boss and knows what is best for us. Whatever the consequences are, deal with them. *Capisce*?

But I couldn't deal. Every day, I asked myself, "How long will this last? Why can't I live a normal life? What have I done to deserve this?"

All I wanted was to live life. Instead, I was living a lie.

What is the theme of Chapter 2?

There is no one single perfect and immutable perception. We live in a world bound by our discrepancies and insecurities. We are all different. It is narcissistic and inhumane to believe that society must reflect your vision and ideology as correct and holy. There is no halo on your head deeming you the chosen one.

Accept, Acknowledge, Embrace!

CHAPTER THREE:

LET THE BATTLE BEGIN

Mazri's Law #3

Never let emotion overrule rationality, unless emotion has a rational justification; only then are you allowed to feel. Until then, you just think with your mind to drive your heart. Do not be a passenger of your own life!

Ready? Fight! Now, it was a fight between just me, myself, and I, as the devils began dancing in my life. At the age of fifteen, I still lived in the middle of nowhere. One hardship after the other was standing in the queue, ready to attack. And what a long queue it was!

My life had taken an ill-defined shape, and only God knew when it would change. My mind was at work twenty-four hours a day, seven days a week, non-stop. I mostly spent my time talking to the four white walls of the living room—though sometimes I talked instead to the walls of my bedroom, as they were more attentive.

I lived an unhealthy routine. My day would start at the high school of condemnation and criticism in the early morning. Then, after school, I would be visited by a thousand thoughts; as I sat on our big blue couch, insecurity would take over. I could hear it ripping away at my soul. When darkness fell, I might stay up all night, my mind working anxiously at my hopes for the future projects, until I'd wear-myself out at about four o'clock in the morning. At other times, I would go to sleep very early in the evening, trying to disconnect myself from reality so I didn't have to feel what I was feeling.

Inside of me, it was pandemonium. There were days when I'd wake up full of hatred for this Hell that was my home, feeling that life was passing me by. I am a vigorous person who loves life's adventures and the people they bring my way. I longed to walk this earth and ascend to the pinnacle of my dreams; surely the view from the top is better. But even when I tried to envision myself in realistic scenarios—sitting with a group of friends by a campfire on a beach, laughing as we pass a bottle around—reality came crashing in. Life had decided to deprive me of its wonders, offering only me its darkest sides when all I wanted was to live.

Depression paralyzed me. I felt incapable of doing the simplest thing—especially when it came to doing the *right* thing. I developed an attitude of indifference, even insolence. What could I gain by being a nice guy? What's the point of kindness? No mercy! Living in this cruel world awakened a monster within me.

Like a prisoner, I was not permitted to leave or re-enter the country

(As if I would want to! Not in a million years!) without an exit and re-entry visa stamped by the Ministry and approved by my Saudi sponsor. I could find no key to unlock the gates of this Hell, nor could I create one. I was doomed!

I had become like a prisoner who counts the days until the end of his sentence, scratching marks on the filthy wall of cement as he stares through the bars; like a prisoner who lives in fear of the assault that can come at any time; like a prisoner.

I listened to the music of Johnny Cash over and over again. The blues in his voice spoke to my soul. Living under religious repression, among people who did not understand or value me, was like serving a life sentence in Folsom Prison. Oh, I was not locked in my room; I had access to a high school education and unlimited family visits. But as in a brick-and-mortar prison, I was isolated from the real world; I spend my precious life at home knitting a long black cape which I might one day use to fly.

Every now and then, I visited my cousins or grandmother, who had become my best friend. We shared laughter, tears, and joy, and celebrated holidays together. This became my only social outlet. When none of them were available, then it was me, myself, and the four walls.

Most days, I simply pivoted from home to school and back. I wandered the house, making a complete circuit more than four times a day, looking for something to do. The boredom was so bad I would actually cry. I'd sit alone in my bedroom, or on the big blue, torn by silent tears until I could barely catch my breath. I'd go outside to take in a bit of fresh air, but the brutal heat would suffocate me, leaving me more breathless than I already was.

I lived my days with tears, confusion, heartache, and breathing problems. My remedy was the red mug of Nescafé—with extra caffeine and four or five spoonsful of sugar—which I had to consume at least twice a day. As it entered my body, I felt a moment of peace, soothing my grief and tears. The caffeine buzz sparked my brain to contemplate how my life would look after my escape from this place. I sat with two fingers pressed to my temple, full of loathing for my present life and full of longing for my future.

The spite that filled me tingled in my blood and nerves. It was almost tangible. As the loathing and longing battled each other in my body, it made me seem arrogant and unapproachable to others. My mother, brother, and sister all perceived me as self-centered. They attempted to talk to me, but I turned them down time and again with a rude remark or a signal to *go away*—leaving me feeling guilty as well as lonely. Deep down inside, I was in desperate need of someone to talk to, but I denied it, lashing out instead.

This is how it started. Here I was, at home, ill-humored like always, sitting on the big blue couch of suede with my Nescafé. I could feel something soft and tender being torn to pieces in my lower chest, at the peak of my stomach. With nothing better to do, I watched *Entertainment Tonight*; even this was out of date. Everything in this Kingdom lagged behind the outside world.

My mom passed by and saw me looking down, frowning. "What's wrong?" she asked me.

"Nothing," I snapped irritably. "*God!*"

She stared, then said, "Then why are you like this?"

I was silent for a moment, and then the truth came rushing out of me like water running down a river of fury. "I cannot take this place. I am fed up!" My voice grew louder. "I go to school, come home, have lunch, maybe a nap, then I wake up to a fight!" The sarcasm was coming thick now. I couldn't help myself. "There's nothing to do but watch TV—and if I don't sleep out the monotony, I might be lucky enough able to see dad in the evening and watch yet *another* family argument. I might even have the chance to join in!"

Mom replied, "It's not like you're here all your life, son."

Before she could say anything else, I cut her off. "Even still, Mom, I feel that I am wasting my life, living in misery."

With that, I burst into tears.

My mother moved in and put her arms around me. "You're ambitious. And you're still very young," she said soothingly. "Soon you will get out and accomplish all your big dreams. Summer vacation is near. You will have a change of atmosphere when we go to Paris, and then we'll stay in Canada a while. Stop crying, son, stop it."

This scene my mother and me would be repeated. She would sense my tiring mind, or hear me roaming in the house. And it was she who bore the worst my harsh and rude behavior. The monster had awakened, and he struck out at the hand of kindness.

Mom was an easy target on whom I could unleash my anger. I was aware that my actions were a kind of wrongdoing, but I found that on some level it satisfied me, when nothing else did.

I also know now that such behavior arises from deep anger and depression—something my parents perhaps didn't know. The cause may have been mysterious to them; otherwise, they didn't take it much into account. Everything has a cause and effect. My family couldn't expect me to act cheerful and pretend everything was all right when I was falling to pieces inside every day.

This had been going on for quite a while. But now it doesn't seem like much to complain about, in comparison with what would come.

What is the theme of Chapter 3?

Never lose self-control or surrender your power to pain, distancing you from your higher self. Have faith in the universal external energy. What you put out there comes right back to you, multiplied by ten! Remember these affirmations: *You can; You could; It's an opportunity;* and *It's possible.* Hold on to the positive mindset you will need to succeed in the biggest battles in life. Think, watch, and see!

CHAPTER FOUR:

POSSESSED HOUSE

Mazri's Law #4

**Boredom is an epidemic disease, fatal
to dreams, innovation, and ambition.
There is always something new to do,
or some habit to undo—
but both require work!**

I have told you how we ended up in our villa in Riyadh. Before the
entire family moved permanently to Saudi Arabia, my parents were in
the Kingdom for a visit, One day, under the dry clouds and fog, they
were driving the wide streets when my mother spotted the house of her
dreams. That night, she wished upon a star for Allah to grant her that
particular white villa.

That prayer was answered three years later, when my dad called us
long-distance to Canada while my mom was pregnant with my baby
brother. The prospect of living in that big two-storey house filled her
with joy, and her excitement was contagious to the rest of us. Upon our
return, my siblings and I were thrilled to select our rooms, decorate

them, and especially visit our Mazri cousins across the street. It seemed like the height of luxury. We had a chauffeur, a housekeeper, front yard, outdoor gym room, and finally the housekeeper's small outdoor room, similar to a pool house. *Cinderella, Cinderella!*

What no one knew is that evil spirits would soon want us out of their home as soon as possible. What was once the beautiful white house would soon turn into a misty grey ruin under a black cloud!

As my teenage years ground on, the Saudi culture and lifestyle continued to take a toll on me. The monotony and unhappiness that settled in my heart had attracted nothing but negative energy to me. I pointed fingers—at the country, and my family—but really, I was the one to blame. I lived in a negative cloud, fomenting family feuds among my parents and siblings. We locked horns like rams, although I was the only Aries in the house. (Astrology could be bunk, but I guess it explains who had the real horns!)

I was not the only one afflicted with boredom. We were all on edge, picking fights over minuscule slights, or even for no reason at all. We grew indifferent and insolent. Everyone was too emotionally drained and mentally fatigued to follow rules in general; it was less work to simply break them.

My emotions overwhelmed my rational thinking. Shouldn't emotions and rationality work in tight harmony? They might, for a more self-aware human being; a well-functioning person can feel with the heart and think with the mind, the two functions working together to choose a course of action.

But I was not functioning well. I didn't understand the idea of "emotional intelligence." I felt like I didn't know much at all. I could barely think straight. All I wanted was to be anywhere but where I was. I wanted out!

One hot night in mid-January, I was sitting in my room as if sitting in prison, but for injustices that I alone perceived. I wept. I wandered back and forth in this room, barely thinking until I found myself picking up the wooden chair from my desk, smashing it against the floor and the wall. My mother and siblings rushed to my room. My mother tried to calm me, but I was wild with anger.

"I'm sick of this place!" I yelled, hitting myself in the face and head. "Enough is enough!"

My mother was afraid I would do myself harm. She called my father at work. My outburst continued until he returned home.

My father stormed in angrily. "Stop it, you fool!" he shouted. "This is absurd!"

I was still furious, but I was more afraid of my father. I gradually brought myself under control. They left me alone and walked down the hall to their bedroom.

I overheard my mother saying, "Let him leave."

"Nonsense," said my father. "He just needs to grow up."

They saw me as a silly child acting out; they failed to empathize with my unhappiness. They claimed that this was where God had put us so that we could live prosperously. This was what was written for us by God since the beginning. They expected *gratitude* from my tired soul and aching heart.

Many parents wish for their children to be as ambitious and

optimistic about their future as I was; but I was in the wrong place at the wrong time for such ambitions. I did not feel acknowledged or appreciated. My family saw me as a troublesome burden—or at least that's how it seemed to me. I was certainly stimulated to anxiety by the feeling that I must make a success of myself, which only added to my depression and anger, as well as my desire to leave as soon as possible in order to become who I want to be.

The red cup of Nescafé no longer brought me relief. Smoking was never an option, as it clashed with my ideal man of physical fitness. I never liked the smell anyway! Drugs were not accessible here, and never caught my attention. However, pills were available in my family circle; my grandmother, uncle, and aunt all used medication to calm their nerves, mainly Ativan (lorazepam), which is used to treat anxiety associated with depression by recalibrating the chemical balance in the brain. Maybe medication could help me.

I had been to the hospital many times with symptoms of anxiety—fainting, rapid heartbeat, breathing problems, or shivering—but no doctor had ever taken me seriously. They considered such a patient's file as humorous and insignificant. "Go play outside," they would say condescendingly. "You'll feel much better." Their lack of consideration frustrated me. Was there anyone out there who could empathize or even sympathize with me? Did anyone understand what I was going through?

It was this place, this country, my home that wounded me so. It is funny when they say "Home, sweet home." There was nothing sweet about it when all I did in this place was *stay home, stay home*. A home symbolizes peace, security, a sense of belonging, and comfort—a place where there is unconditional love that keeps a couple or a family living for each other. But in my house, we barely spoke; we were rarely in the mood. A palpable indifference surrounded us.

And I could scarcely feel secure in a part of the world where the mutaween could ring your doorbell for a provocation as slight as secular music overheard for seconds by your nearest neighbor. The overwhelming feeling was that of residing in a prison. So much for belonging.

Peace isn't born of enforced silence. What erupted in our home almost daily were quarrels, criticism, and family feuds.

My brother and I did not get along very well. He had easily adapted to the Saudi culture of which I so strongly disapproved, causing a clash between us. My mother saw the growing rift between us, and would remind me of how my brother always used to emulate my moves and behavior when we were kids. He would try to get closer to me, but I only retreated.

I was not the best brother. I should have done many things differently, and I have many regrets. I guess it shows how unhappy I was even in childhood, trying to live up to what people thought of me. All of that pressure displaced into hostility toward my siblings. But after our move to Saudi Arabia, if my brother was trying to get closer, it was the worst time to try. I was neither in my most balanced emotional state nor n my best behavior.

Aside from the anguish and depression, my silence was a cause of great distress in the house, driving a wedge between my parents and me. Somehow, saying nothing at all annoyed them; I was considered disobedient. Sometimes a person needs time alone and some personal space, but my parents could not understand that. They could not envision their son passing by them, living under the same roof, while hardly saying "Hello." It seemed disrespectful to them. But I was preoccupied with how I felt. What about respecting my wounded soul?

When I felt blue or in need of a friend to talk to, I had now one to lean on but on my grandmother. She lifted me back up when I fell with her pure and uplifting words. When I talked, she would listen, and when I cried she would tap me on my back gently and soothe me with the wisdom of her soul. The only place I felt I could breathe was at my grandmother's place. She was amazing to be around, as she endorsed laughter, adventure, and a lot of gossip—which was the sole negative side-effect of befriending my granny, since everyone knows the grapevine never leads to any good.

Meanwhile, my father had resigned from his IT company. He had come into legal conflict with his partner over liquid assets worth 8 million Saudi riyals (SAR)—about $2.1 million US—that his Saudi partner had withdrawn from the corporate bank account. My poor father had put all his hard work, sweat, and belief into this company, devoting five years of his life to it and building it into a $5 million company— and in an instant, he lost the value of his shares. (As of this writing, the case is unresolved; my father has won two court actions but the appeal process in ongoing.)

These events triggered grave anxiety in my mother. She had repeated nightmares about malicious supernatural entities inhabiting the house, especially her room. She always felt cold, as though the room she was in were somehow always at a lower temperature than the rest of the house. In the Islamic religion, there are invincible demons who dwell in underground world in the shape of human beings; they can haunt our world, too, much like ghosts—but let's refer to them as *the Others* for now. Some say they appear in the human world to trouble those who are distant from the Islamic faith, or who neglect the religious duties assigned to every human being by Allah.

My mom became convinced that there were two of these Others in the house, and that they were the cause of the shadow hanging over our lives. She consulted the *sheikh*—the religious leader of our mosque— regarding her nightmares and possible presence of supernatural creatures in the house. He kindly urged my mother to play a tape recording of a particular passage from the Quran called *Surat Al-Bakara* ("The Cow"). As the tape played repeatedly, its words became ingrained in my mind.

Indeed, for those who disbelieve, it is all the same for them whether you warn them or do not warn them—they will not believe.

Allah burdens not a person beyond his scope. He gets reward for that (good) *which he has earned, and he is punished for that* (evil) *which he has earned.*

Our Lord! Punish us not if we forget or fall into error, our Lord!

Lay not on us a burden like that which You did lay on those before us (Jews and Christians), our Lord! Put not on us a burden greater than we have strength to bear.

Pardon us and grant us forgiveness. Have mercy on us. You are our Maula (that is, our patron, supporter and protector)*, and give us victory over the disbelieving people.*

The chapter would play in the house over and over again. Saudi Islam has many such customs to drive away bad magic. You might place a blue eye near the entrance of your home to repel jinxes and protect you from envious eyes on your possessions. If you see something you like, you must say *Mash'Allah* (similar to the folk custom in the West of knocking on wood), or the possession that the eye was on will be broken or shattered in some way. The evil eye does not only shatter things but also people, places, and lives.

We tried to act in a more civilized and righteous manner around the house, but I guess at the end it was all pretending. Soon enough, we all came to the breaking point, as monotony affected the entire family—except my father. He despised our nagging and constant complaints about the country. He is not a Saudi by origin, but he said, "This is where Allah has planned for us to be," in a place where he could make the money that was necessary for survival.

In Islam, we believe that nagging attracts negative forces and bad luck, as it demonstrates a lack of appreciation or gratitude for what Allah has given to us. What we fail to value properly, we may lose altogether. We don't realize the real value of our loss or recover from it until genuine appreciation returns. It is like the law of supply and demand, really. And so the world goes round!

Since my mother had started playing the tape, I had begun to pray in my room five times per day. I was seeking positive change and salvation from almighty God. If he created the universe in three days, then he was more than capable of changing my life in a flash. I would cry while I prayed, resting my forehead on the floor, pleading desperately for change: "I believe in your ultimate power and your will, and I turn to you for help." I started reading the Holy Book and being the good boy that any parent would have been glad for their son to be.

However, the angelic character wore off with time. They say the Devil whispers in your ear to discourage you from doing the right thing and obeying God. He will persuade you not to go to gym or will try to discourage you, causing laziness, which in turn weakens the mind. Once you accept and obey his orders, he will sit in the corner and laugh at you, mocking your foolishness and taking pride in his accomplishment. The Devil is evil indeed!

One Thursday night, my mother, sister, and aunt were on their way back home at 9:00 PM with our chauffeur when they were chased. Several Saudi men in a white Bentley and one on a motorbike equipped for the desert crowded the car on the road, spitting on their windows and shouting "I want to fuck you!" over and over again. They pulled in front of our car; my mother locked the doors while my aunt threw a water bottle at the biker's head. In the confusion, the chauffeur managed to reverse and head for home, with the Bentley and bike still in pursuit, while my mother called my father and uncle to the rescue.

As they roared into our street, my uncle came charging out of his house with a baseball bat, running like a madman behind the Bentley. I happened to be outside, about to head off to the gym. My mother screamed for me to come help her from the car. As I hustled her into the house, she turned and flipped off the men with her middle finger.

I turned around to see that the Bentley's windows were up, and all the glass was fully tinted. We couldn't see the owner. He could have been some prince from among the 25,000 princes and princesses in the country. What could we do against a prince? We could easily be deported or sent to jail, if some member of the royal family requested it. They might even stab you dead and get away with it due to their connections.

As the Bentley and the motorcycle vanished in the distance, we were all at home and safe. My father and uncle were actually angrier with the women for not veiling themselves properly, for revealing their glamorous hair and make-up. What a nightmare!

I called our home "the house of burden," because it seemed no hardship would spare us. One after the other was standing in the queue for the Mazri family. No matter how much we tried not to diverge from the righteous path, repelling bad luck and evil spirits, misfortune still befell us.

And still escape seemed an impossible scenario, as if no other country or continent existed. My dad, who had fought all his life to be closer to his family, had important business contacts in the Saudi Arabia, and he felt he was bound to be there; and so we had to live with the daily stress of living in the Kingdom.

Along with depression, monotony, and their side effects, I constantly felt pain in my shoulders and lower back. One day, as I was walking toward the kitchen, my grandmother asked me to stand up straight. She looked at my shoulders with scrutiny and realized that the right one was lower than the left. She immediately grabbed her phone to make me an appointment with her orthopedic doctor.

On Monday evening, we arrived for our doctor's appointment. I was asked to bend down as low as possible (don't try to picture it). The doctor traced his index finger down my spinal cord, starting from my neck and moving lower, bending to the right, curving back to the center and finally to my rectum.

The doctor raised his head. "The boy has scoliosis," he said to my grandmother. "It is a medical condition in which a person's spine is curved from side to side, shaped like an S. The spine may also be rotated. The cause remains unknown, but it is usually inherited."

"That explains it," said my grandma, turning to me. "Your great-grandmother had the same problem."

"I thank her from the bottom of my heart," I grumbled.

My heart sank and my throat went dry as we went back home and broke the news to my parents. My mother and dad both felt my spine. My case was severe enough that the doctor had recommended me for surgery. It was risky; there was a 15 percent chance that I would be left paralyzed. The outcome would largely depend on the surgeon's skills.

I felt as though I had been cursed. Indeed, no hardship would escape me! I went to my bedroom and began to cry, enough tears to fill up the dry bed of Lake Leila. My mother came into the room, sympathetic; she held me while her cold tears fell across my shoulder. I raised my head and told her softly, "I am dying from the inside. I can't go on with my life anymore." My mother continued pouring as many tears as my own. She held me to her chest in a way that seemed to contain me.

On August 28, at 9:00 AM, it was time to head to a private hospital called the Military Hospital. This is where Saudi soldiers and members of the royal family receive medical treatment. I thank the Saudi royal family for their benevolence in paying the full balance of my major surgery, at a cost of SAR 50,000 ($13,500). This gave me access to the best surgeon and hospital in the Kingdom.

In the week leading up to my surgery, I had been completely reserved, emotionally washed and cold in character. My mind had shut down from the misery and simply surrendered, absorbing whatever life brought to it—even if it meant dissecting my back and putting a fifteen-centimeter titanium rod with five solid metal clips against my curvy spinal cord. My body and mind were no longer complaining: I only said, "Whatever."

When the doctor arrived, I was surprised to find that my surgery had been delayed for two more days; there were two more patients ahead of me on the waiting list. I was actually relieved; my fear had started to mount as the time for surgery drew near.

I rose from my bed and went to visit the patient who was next on the list for the surgery. It turned out to be a little girl, six years old, also with scoliosis. Her big brother was in the room keeping her company. She was laughing and playing, but her poor brother's face that spoke of long nights without sleep. But still he kept a smile for his sister's sake. How easy it is to make children laugh, as they appreciate the smallest things in life! It would be so much easier to be like this little girl, not knowing what was to come.

At last, on August 30 at 1:00 PM, all my family—including my uncle, aunt, and grandparents—gathered around my bed, struggling to smile, offering words of wisdom or the assurances of religion—anything to maintain positive energy in the room.

The nurse brought in the surgical bed, and my uncle and father helped to move me onto it. I was injected with anesthesia; I looked into the sad eyes of my mother, searching through her tears for a mother's care. The nurse began to roll the bed toward the elevator and my family followed. My eyes were drooping; my father kept asking, "Did the anesthesia kick in, son? Did the anesthesia . . . ?"

"It's OK," I replied. "Dad, my eyes are closing. Hold my hand."

Mom took my hand. Finally the nurse took me onto the elevator of life and death. I turned my head to see my parents for one last moment while my mother waved goodbye.

My doctor came to greet me and told me that I would wake up as if nothing had happened. He pulled the mask more firmly onto my face; before I knew it, my eyes were completely shut.

It was an escape from the Kingdom. I was free of the sadness buried in my soul. No demons to be found here! No hardship waiting for me. No hurt anymore! I felt good!

I blinked awake to see my brother and father to my right and my mother, uncle, and grandmother to my left. They reached toward me, smiling. "Is my back straight now?" I murmured.

"Yes—and during anesthesia you have said many outrageous things!"

I smiled, but I hoped I hadn't said anything awful about my father while he was present.

"How about the little girl?" I asked.

She was in recovery, just as I would be, crying from the agony in her back. This was the cruelty of scoliosis; before the surgery, there was only a nagging discomfort. Afterward, though—then came the real pain, through which we would have to pass on our way to being fully healed.

My recovery began with a month of bed rest in the hospital. My father would stay up with me all night enduring my silent treatment, mitigated only by my cries of pain. Almost worse than the physical pain was my anger and distress at not being able to walk. Every day, I'd be fitted with a plastic cast buckled down to my back before standing up. I would have to learn how to walk from scratch, as if I had never walked in my life. Each day, I would manage just a few steps before becoming breathless and exhausted. They would take me back to bed; as I rested, I would ponder the importance of gratitude. I used to walk; I used to lift weights. Now I can't do any of these, and I appreciate every single breath I have taken, whether in Sudan, Pakistan, or Saudi Arabia.

Finally, after twenty-five days in the hospital, I was released to go home. It was a great day for all of the family. My mother, sister, and two brothers waited for me outside the garage entrance as the door opened and the Mercedes rolled in. Everything about the house I'd grown so accustomed to now seemed fresh and a little strange, the colors more vivid, the dimensions smaller. And there was my whole family, lined up, wearing joyful faces. I cried with joy as my father helped me down, and I walked the few steps into the house under my own power. My mother hugged me, crying on my shoulders. Suddenly, my three-year-old brother ran toward me, and I cried again, this time from grief because I couldn't pick him up. My recovery was a long way from complete.

My parents had placed my bed downstairs in the second living room, as I would be unable to go upstairs. I would eat, read, talk, write, and drink in bed. Now that was utter monotony! Nevertheless, I refrained from complaining. I simply said, "Thank you, Allah, the most merciful, for everything."

During my recovery, the best of my day was at 7:00 PM, when Oprah Winfrey's TV show ran on MBC 4, a local Middle Eastern English Channel. This amazing woman helped me to rejuvenate my way of thinking, helped me forget my pain with her words of wisdom and the moving stories of her guests.

For six full months, I wore the cast on my body for therapeutic purposes, to protect and realign my back after surgery. My greatest worry was going to high school with this cast wrapped around my body, feeling disabled and untouchable.

The demons had battered my mind and now my body. They had left nothing but threads hanging out of me. Some days I felt worse than death; this third-world country had nearly destroyed me, although I fought for my life like a soldier. But I was still breathing, still surviving—and in one corner of my chest, I felt something alive and beating with delight. My heart was telling me that one day I would be a powerful man, like the ideal man of my imagination—a man worthy of sitting side-by-side with Oprah. As long as I was alive, my future would be bright.

While I was recovering, I wrote a letter to Oprah, resting on my back with my laptop on my stomach.

Dear Oprah,

My name is Nathen and I am an eighteen-year-old who loves hot Oprah. I know it's funny and weird for a teenage guy to be such a big fan of Oprah instead of Snoop Dogg. But life has compelled me to turn toward you—and thank God it did, because it would be a loss to miss a person so full of wisdom.

Oprah, I would like to tell you in a concise way about what you have done for me, and how you have played a great role in my turbulent life. I reside in the Kingdom of Saudi Arabia, where I have spent most of my teenage life feeling like I was in prison. I have been deprived of a social or personal life, and caught up in a sudden culture clash after moving from Canada to this repressive country. It has been a life of tragedy, trauma, depression, conflict, feuds, troubling emotions, a fatigued mind, rage, nervous breakdowns, and other negativities which threatened to make a monster out of me.

In addition to these hot spices on top of my life, I have been through surgery for my spinal cord—seven hours under the knife to correct my scoliosis. Simply put, I had no life; I hardly knew what the word meant, living in this country.

What made my life easier and gave me a reason to survive every single day while going through what no US citizen has gone through is you, Oprah. I have waited not just for your poignant shows but for your innocent soul and erudite mind to advise me what to do, how to deal, and—most importantly—how to live through hard times. I remember vividly sitting on my favorite couch and tearing up as you said, "Patience is sour but then the end it is sweet." It felt like I couldn't wait for that time of fulfillment; I wasn't even sure it was for real.

After my surgery, when I couldn't walk, I used to sit in bed and forget my pain of recovery when you came on. Believe it, Oprah; because you complete me with your words, your heart, and your compassion.

I believe you know that you are a person who cares and has lots to give. I know you get that a lot. But I am a different case—you know why? Because no one loves you as much as I do. I am now writing a book about my tragic life that I want to introduce to the Oprah's Book Club.

Sincerely yours,

Nathen Mazri.

What is the theme of Chapter 4?

Idleness leads to boredom. Lack of vision leads to boredom. Indifference, apathy, lack of ambition—all lead to boredom.

While an oppressive nation may result in a depressed nation, lacking the happiness and productivity necessary to prosper, imagination is the cure for boredom.

Engage in a positive line of thought that inspires rather than causes despair. Suppress a nation, and you shall create rebels; inspire a nation, and you shall create leaders. Monotony is an epidemic affecting millions of lives today, due to the rapid satisfaction of our needs in our technological era, where everything comes easily, resulting in laziness.

Boredom is a negative state of mind. Get up, and do something about it!

CHAPTER FIVE

UNDERSTANDING THE OTHERS

Mazri's Law #5

Empathy is your power to understand why people do what they do, so you can always be ahead of the game. Listen and self-reflect, simultaneously.

The mutawaa walked into a fashion outlet in a mall and aggressively picked up all the T-shirts emblazoned with Buddhas. He threw the shirts rudely at the cashier and watched as he discarded them. Before he left, he pointed his index finger in the face of the Lebanese general manager and said, "It is Allah that we worship, not a brick statue."

It is hard to live in a place where you have to think twice before going out, even to the supermarket—especially when you already have a thousand things on your mind. It's easy to become so preoccupied that you step into a pair of slippers, throw on a cut jersey shirt and shorts, and go out during prayer time, when everything is closed anyway. You stop at a gas station, thinking the place is open; all of a sudden a squad of mutaween in a GMC (thank you, General Motors) come swarming around you, screaming, "Go to prayer, now!" and demanding to see your *iqama*, or residency permit. My strategy was to speak to them in French until they grew bored and left me alone. Piece of cake!

I was *tired*—mentally fatigued, emotionally worn out—and soon I had no love to give because I couldn't find it. I didn't want to feel what I was feeling any longer. I had to put a stop to all this! If I didn't then, no one would do it for me; and all the dreams I had would just drain away. My mother always said, "Don't expect people to come and save you. Your father and I can only do so much."

In considering my trouble fitting in here in Saudi Arabia, I had begun to wonder if the fault was mine. Perhaps I was the ignorant one; perhaps, instead of being indifferent to the culture's mentality, I should blame myself for failing to respect the behavior and attitudes of my peers. Canadian values were engraved in my mind. The norms were so different from those here in the Kingdom. But Canada was far away; I had to let go and move on. Life itself was the biggest school, and I had the opportunity for a new discovery, a new learning journey! What if I started opening up to the culture, to the people—to life?

Step by step, I started to tolerate and learn patience. I would not live forever in Saudi Arabia; I determined to find the good in the country while I waited. I still longed to leave behind a life of mindless obedience, to leave behind the criticism I faced daily at school; but I waited. I still longed to be loved one day by another human being, to earn the love and respect of my father, to heal and to walk again, to belong to a worthwhile group of friends . . . and life in the waiting room went on.

Most middle- and upper-class Saudi households have two or three domestic servants to help with day-to-day tasks. Typically, this household staff will include at least one housekeeper and often a chauffeur; the latter is indispensable because women are not permitted to drive. Many Saudi children, therefore, grow up expecting to get what they want when they want it, even if it is just a glass of water; they need only ask, and a servant will fetch it for them, wherever they are in that big villa. Parents do not prepare their children for how the world really works. Materialism runs rampant; a child will not have the chance to experience unconditional love. Parents are a child's biggest influence, but Saudi parents—who have themselves been overindulged their whole lives—often fail to model good values. How can a child learn patience and humility for their children when all the adults he sees expect to be waited on wherever they go? As soon as a Saudi customer walks into a store, he or she expects immediate service, even if the salesperson is already helping someone else. The Saudi citizen must be answered at all times.

One weekend after the gym, I was waiting in line at a Second Cup coffeeshop. Just as I was about to place my order, a Saudi man, milky dark and slightly overweight, suddenly barged in front of me and started ordering. *Hello-o-o! Excuse me! I am alive! How can anyone think this is acceptable? Does he think this is obedient and mannerly conduct? At his age, what is he thinking?*

I asked myself then: How is it that I know the difference between good and bad manners, and he doesn't? With time, I understood that I had been taught discipline and etiquette in early childhood, in many small ways, without even realizing it. In my first-grade classroom, at St. Norbert, Laval, Montreal, the teacher told me not to walk on my tiptoes: "God gave you an entire foot," they said. "Use it." I learned the three "magic words": *please*, *thank you*, and *I'm sorry*. I learned to wait my turn in the queue without pushing or shoving, how to share, and many other little things. These simple lessons are rarely taught to children in the Middle East.

Ego plays a great role for the Syrians and Lebanese. The attitude that starts from youth is "Look at me! Don't you know who I am?", and it continues growing in adulthood. It was clear to me just by the way these men talked and carried themselves that they used their ego to mask their insecurities.

Ego is found everywhere, and on reflection I was displeased to find it even in myself. I, too, was spoiled, and considered the people in this country as beneath me. That was my biggest chronic negative perception. Everything the Arabs did was different from what I was used to—how they ate, how they lad their lives, how they thought, how they treated others. Everything about them was against who I am. Hence, I could not tolerate the culture one bit!

But I couldn't bring the entire culture over to my way of thinking. So I had to learn to give way gracefully where I could—to let things go, to tolerate, and seek to understand rather than condemn. Instead of making enemies, I would seek to build relationships; you never know who can benefit you.

Walking in the mall one afternoon, I saw a group of girls, looking like so many black bags of coal under their *abayas*. They started giggling and wandering around me. As I walked on, a piece of white paper was thrown before me on the floor. Being the decent man I am, I picked it up to put it in the garbage; I unfolded the paper and saw a Blackberry PIN and a number. I smiled—it was nice to receive attention—but then tossed it in the trash. I wasn't interested!

I didn't blame the women, of course. They had no place to socialize, network, or flirt, no real outlet for human nature. At this time, most girls, before going out, had to ask permission from their older brother or father who acts as a *mohram*, or guardian. Any man accompanying and unmarried girl in public is a relative, sibling, or father—a man who can't be a sexual partner.

In recent years, the law has been liberalized. It is no longer legally required for a girl to be accompanied by a *mohram*; but many families still follow the custom. Sometimes I think Saudi Arabia might be becoming a little more lenient year by year, until I find myself followed by mutaween. When that happens, I stop thinking these positive thoughts, as experience seems to be proving me wrong.

As I approached my last year in Saudi Arabia, I received conditional acceptance from Concordia University in Montreal, where I hoped to pursue my bachelor's degree in marketing. The university would need the CITA accreditation verification from my high-school, SABIS International School, or King Abdul-Aziz International School, before my acceptance could be finalized. I thought that would be easy, yet when I went to my English teacher and asked her for such a letter, she replied that she couldn't help me; I would need to go to the principal's office.

And so I did, where I proceeded to get into a stressful argument with the Lebanese secretary, who obviously had a problem with me. Now, obviously I had my problems with the Saudi culture and mindset, but dealing with Lebanese brought a whole new set of difficulties. To understand the Lebanese, think the movie *Mean Girls*, with Lindsay Lohan; jealousy, materialism, hatred, and gossip flow among them, overwhelming you with negative energy. I can feel it plainly, perhaps because my spirit is not resistant to such energy. Dealing with vicious gossip taught me one valuable thing, at least: to develop a thick skin and not care about other people's opinions—because if you do, good luck living a happy life constantly worrying about what *he* said, or what *she* thinks about you...

Finally, I walked into the principal's office and asked him for the CITA confirmation. He replied that the school was not yet accredited. I was in a state of shock. I felt lied to, gullible; the school had a CITA logo displayed in their marketing materials, and we had taken it at face value—but it was sham. My ticket out of the country was in tatters.

I stormed out of the office, filled with anger. Coming back late into the classroom, I grabbed my things and left, with no regard for the consequences. I went home, driving my blue MINI Cooper—a gift from my father and his Saudi partner—and explained the situation to my parents. They were as angry as I was.

It seemed there was nothing I could do. The old bad feeling of being trapped came back at full force. In misery, I turned the TV to *The OC*, a program about American high-schoolers. This was how life was what supposed to be, I thought: young people go to school, they get their prom, they graduate; lovers apply to the same college, get accepted, and life goes on.

But not for me! My life is always a fight. It is a battle! But the question was: who was I against? Unlike those American students, I had to appeal to Saudi the Ministry of Education to certify my report card. Struggling for my future, I was forced to place my hopes and dreams in the hands of these conservative Bedouins.

I had been struggling to develop more empathy and understanding for the culture around me. But discovering the extent of the corruption in the educational system, with international schools falsely claiming to be accredited, reignited my prejudice against the Arabs.

My father always admonished me to stop saying "Arabs this, and Arabs that." I told him I had no reason to think otherwise; I was crushed into pieces, trying to find my present and future. But he was right; if we took it out on a whole culture every time we had a conflict, it would be a World Civil War. Better to rely on the essential human qualities—self-awareness, self-control, introspection, and empathy—to resolve conflicts and enhance cooperation, especially in business.

I had been dealt a setback, but I moved forward. I had to transfer to a different school, an accredited school that will remain unnamed here. The administration sympathized with my situation over the last semester, and I was allowed to transfer immediately before final exams week. The principal agreed to transfer my grades from my final semester at my previous school; however, I was given the chance to take the exams anyway, on the chance that I might raise my final grade with a good exam score. I didn't, sadly—but I was moved by the kindness of the gesture. Good people existed in this country, sympathetic people with generous hearts—if you only believed.

And that is the best lesson I had learned: hope for the best! If you think negatively, you will attract negativity; if you think positively, you will attract similar energy. In my darkest days, I had felt that one hardship after another was out to get me. I never gave myself a break. Being pampered from a young age, I felt the world revolved around me; so if I suffered, I felt sure the world was determined to make me suffer. But what if it was nothing personal all along? Before understanding the culture, I had to understand myself. It was the hardest lesson in my life—to understand me.

I was busy creating the ideal world inside my head where one day I would belong. I had no sense of self-belonging, neither in Saudi Arabia nor even, truly, in Canada. My real home country, Palestine—land of my ancestors—was a battleground. The Al-Aqsa Intifada, which began in 2000, raged throughout my youth, and every day there were more gruesome images of dead children, grieving mothers, and destruction. The most infamous broadcast image came on October 2, 2000, when the BBC reported that a Palestinian father and son had been caught in the crossfire between Palestinian security forces and Israeli troops. For forty-five minutes, Jamal al-Durrah tried in vain to shield his son Mohammed from gunfire as they crouched against a concrete wall near Netzarim, in the Gaza Strip. The whole scene was caught on camera by a cameraman from France's Channel 2, and was played repeatedly on Palestinian television. The father was seen desperately to Israeli troops, shouting "Don't shoot!" But the terrified boy was hit by four bullets and collapsed in his father's arms. Al-Durrah, though badly wounded, said his son died for "the sake of Al-Aqsa mosque," the holy site in Jerusalem seen by the Palestinians as both sacred and sovereign territory. The story was retold endlessly on Al-Jazeera, Al-Arabiya, CNN, the BBC, and dozens of other channels worldwide, and made a deep impression on me. War was an everyday subject in Middle Eastern life.

Clearly, I had not led a normal adolescent life so far! Understanding myself around these intolerable others was a challenge. I had an idealized vision—largely drawn from American teen movies—of how my life *should* be. Every piece of the puzzle had to fall into place, and nothing else would satisfy me. I needed a group of friends I could go to the theatres with; a lover I could tease in the school hallway; a road trip every weekend in someone's convertible; a friend to jog with me every morning and evening; and finally, a big dream to pursue—and achieve, knowing I live in the land of opportunities. Quite a list of demands! But to me, they seemed like basic lifestyle necessities.

But youth culture in the Kingdom was nothing like my imaginary teen movie. Driving on Tahleyah Street, the "main drag" in Riyadh—some call it the Champs-Elysees of Saudi Arabia—was a never-ending traffic jam of teenage Saudis stopping their cars in the middle of the street to wave the flag of the Al-Hilal football club. We would simply wait for them to drive forward. Buggies and motorcycles made their way aggressively in the middle of the street, and even performed amateur stunts on the sidewalks. The police did nothing to stop them; in fact, they seemed to be enjoying the show.

Looking at these teenagers would simply fill me with disgust for their misbehavior. Where was the law? The police did nothing to stop them; in fact, they seemed to be enjoying the show.

I only started to get past my loathing when I considered whether these young men here were really responsible for their own actions. If the country's regulations suppressed freedom and prevented them from pursuing many of a human being's normal social needs, then the Saudi citizens of tomorrow were as much victims as I was—raised with a limited and narrow mentality, and with little hope for the future. They, too, were full of rage at their boring lifestyles, but they channeled it outward into such behaviors as racing on the street of Tahleyah, or following girls in their window-tinted GMCs. Boys will always be boys, and no country can change human nature. It is easy to change someone's behavior, but difficult to change their attitudes. We were really all in the same boat; even though I found their actions intolerable, I understood that they, too, were reacting against their environment.

It was an environment with little respect for human rights—but even here, there was some cause for hope. On June 3, eighteen members of the mutaween were detained after coming under heavy pressure following for the deaths of two people in their custody in less than two weeks. The Saudi government's National Society for Human Rights, established in 2004, issued a report criticizing the behavior of the religious police; and in May 2006, the Interior Ministry issued a decree stating that "the role of [the CPVPV] will end after it arrests the culprit or culprits and hands them over to police, who will then decide whether to refer them to the public prosecutor." Until that point, mutaween had enjoyed broad powers to arrest, detain, and interrogate those suspected of moral infractions. This marked a beginning of a long-overdue change, though we are still a long way from implementing all necessary reforms.

The oppressive regulations of the Kingdom are meant to promote a godly lifestyle; but the citizens of this Islamic paradise flee abroad whenever they can. Even though the cost of living in Riyadh is six times lower than in London, Saudis fly to Great Britain every week. Twenty-five airlines operate between London and Riyadh, with 179 flights per week. British Airways alone has service five times a week from both Riyadh and Jeddah. They go to indulge in their fantasies of all the liberal world has offer—things regarded as sinful in Islam. I do not blame these citizens! They only want the right to live, to indulge and forget their worries. Let them act on their forbidden desires, be carried away by temptation without thinking twice, mingle and flirt with the opposite or same se; let them be themselves, comfortable in their own skins, and wear cut shirts or fashionable garments without being stalked by mutaween.

But Saudis are hesitant about reforms at home. I was sitting one day with a wealthy young Saudi—he worked for a jewelry company—who told me, "I don't want to see Saudi Arabia become liberal. It is good to sin overseas and come back home clean, godly, and ready to work." I can understand this way of thinking; caught up between religion and life's temptations, they seek this balance. Sinful pleasure is just a short plane ride away, but in their everyday lives they can feel free from temptation. As soon as they return to the Kingdom, they can feel psychologically clean from their sinful acts. I understand that they wouldn't want to see Saudi Arabia become more westernized, where the country's Generation X already emulates MTV.

Even if it were the will of the people, though, reform would be a difficult proposition. A vast democratic gap exists. The people's voices are scarcely heard—particularly the voices of Saudi women; unseen and unheard, with limited human rights, their pain and voices re swept aside by the men in power. That is another story, and one that is not mine to tell. In most cases, Arabs have learned to live with boundaries; they live within limits and dream within limits. They believe in reason over passion and reality over dreams. People like me—we are the dreaming rebels of the family. They are raised this way. Their parents expect them to become the best in their field; not the field that sparks their passion, but one that bring them to the highest peak of bourgeoisie—medicine, the law, engineering—career choices that guarantee very good livelihoods and a good standard of living that their parents didn't enjoy, especially if they lived through the 1948 Palestinian–Israel War and didn't have the opportunity to migrate overseas.

Saudi Arabia itself, though, did not live through such wars. There were no military jets battling over their grand cement palaces. But the Kingdom's economic and cultural development in the postwar era has lagged behind that of the west. Coming to Saudi Arabia from Canada, I was (perhaps foolishly) expecting the same quality of life, the same freedoms and rights, the same architectural diversity, and all the same opportunities available in the great land of dreams. Never set your expectations too high, or you will be traumatized by reality.

Even in Saudi Arabia, there has been progress and change. Well int the twentieth century, the country was practically a medieval kingdom, bound by the precepts of Wahhabism, a puritanical religious movement within Islam that was founded more than 300 years ago. Until fairly recently, public life in the Kingdom of Saudi Arabia has been dominated by this form of Islamic belief and its mission to stamp out impurities; but after an inside look at modern Saudi life it is clear that many citizens have grown out of it. They still keep true to their religion in its core tenets, praying five times a day, fasting during Ramadan, and giving the 2 percent *zakat* every year. A growing number of modern young Saudis have given up even these practices; though they still consider themselves Muslims, they do not perform the daily *wudu* (ritual cleansing) and prayer. Even in this conservative culture, where suppression, restrictions, and obligations still abound, more people are exercising the power of choice.

You are what you set yourself to become. "Limits" did not exist in my vocabulary until I learned the real definition in the hardest way possible. I was bound to stay at home with my 2 kg plastic-and-gypsum cast on my torso, lying in my bed in the living room, kicking and crying as the pain from my surgery broke my sleep. I cried in the moonlight through the window as father rushed to console me, massaging my feet to help me fall asleep. For endless nights, my father would show me the same care; and years before, this same father had shown me insensitive and unsupportive chastisement as I struggled with teenage trauma and depression.

But that night, the love he had inside him for me became visible. I could see it in his beaten eyes, which reflected his beaten oldest son. I knew that night that he had simply been doing the "father" job in order to make me stronger and thicker-skinned—the man he had long sought for me to become. But with time, he would come to comprehend that I would become very different from the picture of me he had held in his mind. Again, we see the power of expectations; I truly believe it is the high expectations for which we train our minds that drive us to become unhappy. Expectations are the driving force of dissatisfaction and unhappiness. One must not sit there and expect results, but instead inspire change and results.

I tried to empathize with my father, to understand the forces that had shaped his attitude toward me. Was it was the way he was raised by my grandparents? Had he had a father-and-son bond with my grandfather? Or perhaps it was the fact he had lived through the 1982 Lebanon War that had made him so tough and cold-hearted—or so he seemed to me. Or was it that he had gotten married in his late teens? Those years were hard; my grandmother resented my mom at first, and my father—only eighteen years old—went through the hardship of mediating between them, while working hard to earn a living and take care of his first son, myself. Did he expect me to follow his footsteps, or did he simply want me to become that version of a man he had engraved in his mind for me? He knew very well that the country had been hard on me, and the culture clash was slapping me on both cheeks with no mercy. But he couldn't understand or empathize with my situation; he called me a complainer, and unappreciative.

With my new, hard-won patience, however, it came: *appreciation.* This was the lesson with the largest number of chapters. Its endless doctrines pounded my tired skull as I attempted to comprehend the true meaning and value of this twelve-letter word. I remembered the words of my grandmother, who has always been my shoulder to lean on. "Look below you and say, 'Thank you, God,'" she said. "Then look above you and say '*Inchallah!*'"—that is, "God willing."

It is always when you are about to lose something that you start to appreciate its value. After three years in this grand white villa, we began to be financially shaken when my father when my father—as mentioned in chapter 4—was betrayed by his business partner. The business lessons I learned from a young age would stand me in good stead if I ever thought of working here, but I had absolutely no plans coming back. Business in Saudi Arabia works differently from anywhere else in the world. If you wish to open any kind of business as a foreign investor, you must put up an initial investment of more than $100,000, and there are endless supporting documents and government red tape. (This in a country where government corruption is endemic; Transparency International's annual Corruption Perceptions Index, which rates countries on a scale from 0 (highly corrupt) to 10 (highly clean), gave Saudi Arabia a score of 4.7 in its 2010 survey.)

Most problematically, any foreign investor who wishes to open a business in Saudi Arabia must partner with a Saudi citizen. This requirement creates a power imbalance between Saudi investors and foreign entrepreneurs, leaving outsiders vulnerable to exploitation. Even if all the know-how comes from outside the country, the local partners—who bring nothing but money and regulatory legitimacy to the table—still hold rigid expectations. Some Saudi partners won't even put up any money of their own; they'd rather take a percentage in exchange for giving you access, registering your business under their name and their bank authority. You take all the financial risk, and they reap the benefits. The gap in business culture also makes it difficult to increase the number and skill level of Saudi investors and entrepreneurs with international ties.

Another quirk of Saudi business culture is that Arabs generally love to do business with people of similar interests and culture. No matter how close you are, you will never be safe! Deals are mostly political and based on personal relationships; this can work to your advantage, if the local investor starts working his magic on your behalf among his contacts. Decisions can take a long time; a client might ask for a proposal or contract, and six months or more could pass before he makes the decision to lay out his first payment. With patience (that's a virtue), coupled with flexible and laid-back persistence, you will certainly reap the reward.

Arabs will also speak in vague terms during negotiations; it is up to the entrepreneur to nail down all the necessary specifics, or bear the responsibility. The way you talk—even your body language—can affect your entire business. You should always be able to handle requests, assume blame, and flatter your Saudi client—especially if he has a 50 million-riyal payment in fifteen days. You are up for a Spartacus challenge!

Finally, business visas can be difficult to obtain. They are issued at the discretion of the Ministry of Foreign Affairs, and of the local embassies and consulates. You may think you have all the paperwork in place for a six-month, multiple-entry business visa—but when you open your passport, you find it stamped with a visa for only thirty days! Letters of Invitation now come electronically via the Saudi Ministry of Foreign Affairs web site, and invitations must originate from reputable companies in Saudi Arabia. Officially backed companies tend to have fewer problems getting people into the Kingdom. There are a lot of hoops to jump through—but once you get in, the Saudi market can be extremely lucrative.

With financial disappointment on the horizon, the tired souls of my family were all crying out, waiting desperately for circumstances to change so we could leave this country. At the same time, we did not wish to see our standard of living drop—especially my mother, who had endured the Canadian lifestyle with my father for more than eleven years. In Canada, there would be twice the struggle for every dollar before taxes. Tough life! But we had to weigh these considerations against the difference in our lifestyles in the two countries. We had to understand the power of our want. We had to understand where our real happiness lay. We were obliged to go through a journey of self-understanding to determine we really wanted from life. We certainly couldn't live in poverty, so there had to be an answer.

For my father, though, the decision was already made; we would stay on in Saudi Arabia, secure our life, and strive for the riches. That's when we learned money wasn't everything! We were torn, sick, troubled, angry, bored, lifeless, and depressed. Joy was a hard a ride to get on.

Being in the Islamic region of the world, it was normal for us to seek inspiration or comfort in the teachings of our faith. Desperately seeking for an answer—or for hope—we listened attentively to our religious friends, consulted my grandfather, and watched the religious programming on the satellite channel Iqraa, divining what could be the truth!

I, out of everyone, was the least religious and most rebellious. I was overzealous and wanted to be many things at once—actor, creative director, entrepreneur, and wealthy philanthropist, either all at the same time or consecutively. I was fascinated by the kind of man who accumulates wealth. For me, it was an art—the art of wealth. My imagination was energized to generate many business ideas and plans, all of which were stacked in my bedroom drawer.

For a *sheikh* to sit me down and explain the limitations on my horizons was hard for me to accept. But I was looking for answers, and would take them anywhere I found them. I was bound to listen if the sheikh talked sense; let's face it, I am a Muslim when all is said and done. I had my beliefs, and limited understanding, but my religious knowledge was immature. When I was a teenager, I didn't go to spring break parties or on road trips to Las Vegas; I slept over at my grandparents' house for a change of atmosphere. And it was there that I

heard from my grandfather the Islamic doctrines and legendary stories
whose valuable morals so took me by surprise. I shook my head with
dubious arguments, while my grandfather fixed the missing puzzle
pieces for me as if he'd played this game a thousand times before.

In the summer rain of Montreal city, I woke up to the sound of
crying from the next room. Pushing away the bed covers, I stampeded
to my mother's room. She was crying on her bed with the phone in her
hand; my aunt had called the announce the death of my grandfather, the
man who had such an influence on all our lives—especially on mine.
He had been hospitalized before we left for our vacation in Canada; his
last words to my mother before our departure were "Take care of
Nathen for me." He knew the hurt I was feeling. He felt it in my soul,
and saw it in my eyes, he witnessed breaking bones, and he forecasted
my forthcomings. And now he was gone.

I cried for days, barely rising from my bed in my despair and
listlessness. I thought, *Is this life? We are born, we suffer, we laugh, we
cry, we sacrifice, we teach, we love, and we die. What if my mother is
next? What if I am next?*

I realized there is no escape from death. I vowed to leave this Earth
with my footprint in the ground and a story to be told for the new
generation. I would someone of wisdom and success. If we are all
going to die, then I might as well leave with a voice.

But all this was easier said than done. I felt imprisoned in a place
where I didn't want to be, but pressured by family to accept that this
was where the money and opportunities were, in the land of a fast-
booming developing economy, where so much was possible—even if

you were utterly unhappy. They believed I was still too young to make the best decision for myself. It's tough for a twenty-one year-old man to withstand an independent life financially and emotionally; they were right about that—especially the finance part! However, they believed in me—in my intelligence and my strength of character. I had strong opinions about the Arab world, and my parents knew they couldn't change that. I was raised in the west, after all; and besides, most of the statements I made about the Arabs were true, however biased and critical. The prospect of financial security was the only thing that bound me to Saudi Arabia, given our proximity to the El-Masri family and relatives.

The Politics of the Kingdom

Arabs are big talkers, not doers. They over-promise and under-deliver; they make appointments and always arrive late. The Lebanese politicians you see talking on the Arab news are constantly in conflict. They do not speak with proper decorum; their foul language is shameful on public television. The dictatorships that reigned for more than fifty years in Libya, Syria, Tunisia, and Iraq—some of which are still in power—fostered tyranny and turmoil, which has warped the minds of Arab men, encouraging them to obsess over masculinity and manliness, and driving many to think of dominance as the right path, when in fact it is humanity that is most important. Arabs value the rights of men, rather than human rights. The repressive regimes of Syria and Saudi Arabia, in particular, are notorious for their lack of consideration for human rights.

Saudi Arabia is one of around thirty nations on the planet with legal lashing and judicial corporal punishment. In Saudi Arabia's case this encompasses amputation for burglary and lashing for lesser crimes, such as "sexual deviance" and drunkenness, even tipsiness. The number of lashes is not codified in law; the exact punishment is assigned at the judge's discretion, and may range from a few dozen lashes to many hundreds, typically doled out over a period of weeks or months.

In 2004, the UN Committee Against Torture criticized Saudi Arabia over its use of amputations and floggings. The Saudi delegation reacted by citing "lawful conventions" in place since the founding of Islam 1,400 years ago, and dismissing the criticism as obstruction of the government's legitimate authority. Saudi Arabia likewise practices the death penalty, including open executions by decapitation. Beheading is the punishment for magicians, traitors, spies, terrorists, apostates, murderers, rapists, drug traffickers, and armed robbers, as per strict interpretation of Islamic law. In 2008, Saudi Arabia carried out 102 executions—more than any other nation except China.

A representative for Saudi Arabia's National Society for Human Rights has said that numbers of executions are rising because wrongdoing rates are rising, that detainees are dealt with sympathetically, and that the decapitations act as a deterrent to crime. "Allah, our designer, knows best what's useful for His people," said the spokesman. "Should we simply consider and protect the privileges of the killer, and not think about the privileges of others?" Saudi Arabia has blocked access to the website of Amnesty International after the organization leaked a draft of a proposed Saudi anti-terrorism law that would impose harsh punishments for political dispute or even study of the imperial gang.

Saudi women face segregation in various ways in their lives—for example, the equity framework. Despite the fact that they comprise 70 percent of those enrolled in colleges, women, for social reasons, make up just 5 percent of the workforce in Saudi Arabia; that is the lowest ratio of any country. The treatment of women has been characterized as "sex politically-sanctioned racial segregation." or "gender apartheid."

The organization Women2Drive waged a campaign via Facebook and Twitter to urge women to follow the example of Najla Hariri and Manal Al Charif and defy the prohibition against women driving by getting behind the wheel on June 17. Manal, one of the founders of Women2Drive, was arrested for driving her car in Khobar, in the eastern part of the Kingdom. How ironic for a Muslim country to prohibit a woman's rights when the Quran states, "O you who believe! You are Forbidden to inherit women against their will…" (Quran 4:19) A corrupted social order—*not* Islam itself—is the problem.

The criminal code also regards homosexuality and cross-dressing as offenses, and conventional social mores tend to view such behavior as debauched and immoral. The most extreme punishment for "sexual abnormality" is beheading, but the courts have the discretion to opt for lesser punishments, including fines, lashing, detention, and deportation. By law, any Saudi citizen diagnosed with HIV or AIDS is qualified with the expectation of complimentary restorative consideration, insurance, and career opportunities. Yet hospitals will refuse treatment to infected patients, especially expats and foreign guest workers, who will be immediately deported. Numerous schools and clinics are hesitant to distribute government data about the virus, and HIV remains associated with shame and disgrace throughout the Gulf region.

Until the late 1990s, data on HIV/AIDS was not broadly accessible to people in general, but this has begun to change. In the late 1990s, the Saudi government recognized World AIDS Day and permitted data about the virus to be distributed in daily papers. The exact number of individuals living in the Kingdom who had been diagnosed remained a firmly guarded secret. In 2003, the government declared the number of cases of HIV/AIDS in the nation to be 6,700; that number had risen to more than 10,000 in June 2008. Condoms are accessible in doctors' offices and drugstores, even in a few supermarkets—but purchasing them remains shameful.

To date, Saudi Arabia does not have any sort of reasonable human rights laws. Saudis have a religious tax, the *zakat*, that requires all Muslims to give no less than 2.5 percent of their wage to non-profit foundations, and a great number of these philanthropies are genuinely devoted to great aims. However, beheading is still practiced on Fridays. Why would I want to live in a country of Iron Age laws when I am a Canadian citizen? Is it the money that I am making that is keeping me patient and quiet?

The Settlers

Arabs are not risk-takers; they are settlers. They are not trend-setters, but rather trend-followers. They wish to make high salaries, support their family and kids, and pay the bills. And while that's all well and good, many crave a more lavish lifestyle, thinking they are Marie Antoinette at Versailles. Snobs over who has visited the west more often, or who attended a western university, or who speaks better English—and if you have managed all of the above, get ready to be torn with hatefulness.

Arabs are greatly inspired by the west, and though they say they despise American politics or the Bush administration, I believe it is best they focus on their own administration . . . Oh wait! They don't have one. Lebanon is corrupt and the rest of the Middle East consists of dictatorships where the people have nothing. In Egypt, for example, 80 percent of the population lives on just $2 per day, according to the World Bank statistics. At least they are known to talk rather than execute.

From a marketing and advertising perspective—my own specialty—when did Arabs create brands consumed globally, rather than buying Western brands such as Louis Vuitton, Giorgio Armani, or Nike and visiting restaurants like McDonald's, Baskin-Robbins, Chili's, Applebee's, and Le Notre? Arabs are not trend setters, they are trend followers; but even here, they take much more time to follow up than the rest of the world. They never stand in a queue and always push themselves through aggressively, like a crowd of starving refugees after a bowl of rice. I wonder where the civilization is. This shows that there is no proper system of governance in the country to set an example for the people.

If you meet Saudi officials, you soon realize that many of them are actually Western-educated liberals. The oil minister, for instance, went to Lehigh and Stanford. The former ambassador to the United States attended University of North Texas and Georgetown. Before 9/11, more than 60,000 Saudis came to the United States each year. That number has dropped to around 25,000. Still, in 2006, more than 11,000 visas were issued to incoming Saudi students. Think most of those kids don't absorb American culture and values while they're in college? Many of them go back and become high-ranking officials in Saudi Aramco or the government.

Finally, I do not find the young men's and women's behaviors and attitudes reprehensible when the society has suppressed them from their freedom, leisure time, temptation—even from their natural feelings of love, as their life-long partner is chosen by the father at all times, especially when it comes to their daughters. A close friend of mine, a young Saudi woman of twenty-four, went home to find out that her father had arranged a meeting with his friend and the friend's son— who had come to take both of his daughters. Yes, both—one for the son and the other daughter (aged twenty-one) for the father! Shockingly true.

There are numerous instances of *adhl,* or the act of keeping a woman single against her will; some have made their way to Saudi courts. One of the best-known cases involved a forty-two year-old surgeon. She had received numerous offers of marriage; however, her dad has turned every one of them down, while taking her paychecks for himself.

"A Saudi lady can't purchase a telephone without the guardian's authorization," said Al-Hawaidar, who has been banned from composing or appearing on Saudi TV or radio as a result of her vocal advocacy of women's rights. "This law keeps women as adolescents who can't be responsible for themselves; they are treated as juvenile, and in the meantime it gives all the power to men."

In a recent report by the *Al-Hayat* daily newspaper, the National Society for Human Rights investigated 30 cases of *adhl* this year—and this figure is more than likely an undercount. A Facebook group called "Enough Adhl," set up by a college teacher who is herself an *adhl* casualty, estimates the true number at almost 800,000 cases. The group, which has 421 members, advocates for harsher punishments against men who abuse their guardianship. An estimated 4 million women over twenty years old are unmarried in a nation of 27 million.

According to Human Rights Watch, Saudi judges have repeatedly granted fathers the right to interfere arbitrarily in their adult children's private lives, in serious violation of their right to privacy and to establish families freely. Fathers have imprisoned their adult daughters for "disobedience," prevented them from marrying, and been granted custody over a grandchild without valid reason—all with the support of the courts. In November 2009, and again in August 2010, Human Rights Watch wrote to the governmental Human Rights Commission of Saudi Arabia regarding the cases of two Saudi women whose brothers forced them to marry multiple men against their will, and who suffered physical, sexual, and verbal abuse in their family homes.

It's only common decency for a young Saudi man to obey his father, rather than scolding and yelling that he can do whatever he wants as he isn't a child any longer. It's simply disrespectful for him to say, "You can't tell me what to do anymore," then stumbling out the door with his girlfriend, leaving the father embarrassed. That may be how the American father-and-son relationship works; but in Saudi Arabia the children sit with their father until he goes to bed, and they sit down at the table only after their father has taken his seat. They fear their father's anger bursting out, and so they try to obey at all times. There's an argument to be made that this dynamic among Saudi families helps keep relationships solid by rooting them in respect. In any case, Saudi Arabia—unlike many western societies—is spared the problem of runaway youth falling into homelessness, drug abuse, and sexual exploitation. We can learn from Saudi families if we examine the dynamics at play, which keep families together and foster close relationships.

The late King Abdullah, who reigned from 2005 until his death in 2015, was a radical modernizer by Saudi standards. He wanted to encourage more contact with the outside world, and to project an image other than one of religious austerity. But it's a hard sell. Visas these days for westerners are so scarce that even top American diplomats have a hard time obtaining them for family members.

There is, however, an American military presence in the country, but they don't exactly feel welcome here. I hear from my friend Aron—a New Yorker who worked here as an English professor at the King Saud University before taking a job at the US military compound known as "The Rock"—that the Americans in the compound believe the whole world is against them. I wonder why? When they leave the compound to go outside in Riyadh city, they are told to travel in groups at all times, in case they are attacked. They lead their lives with this notion that they are always under the world's eye. Perhaps it's a sign of a guilty conscience.

There is a travel magazine called *Ahlan Wasahlan,* meaning "Hello and Welcome," but the welcome seems to be to Versailles, Provence, and Belize. There's no hint that Saudi Arabia itself might be a destination. It's a great place for the airline industry, because so many citizens want out: anywhere but here.

Saudi Arabia is the only country in the world that technically works for only six business months—January to June—with the other six months consisting of summer holidays, Ramadan, and Eid. But if you think this would make it a leisure destination, think again. They call this the Forbidden Country. The Kingdom recoils at the thought of the culture clash that could be caused by an invasion of French girls in shorts and American boys with joints. A sign at the airport warns, "Drug traffickers will be put to death." It's the most bewildering vacation spot you'll never vacation in, due to the extreme red tape for tourist visas. Would you like to do a little shopping during your visit? You'd better check the time; the mutaween still roam the streets to ensure that all stores close their doors during prayer time. If you wear revealing clothes or have an indecent "western look" (e.g., sleeveless shirts, long hair, piercings), you may be harassed. Even McDonald's has two sections, to keep men and women separate. (I guess it's a Big Mac for men and Big Mrs. for women!) Young men throw paper leaflets with their mobile phone numbers onto the windshields of cars where girls ride. International schools are all divided by gender—male and female—where same-gender individuals grow together as long as they both shall live. Monotony, depression, anxiety, rage, and stress are facts of life for many young men and women.

However, I was proud to see on the MBC channel a PSA about terrorism declaring, "I am Muslim: I am against terrorism." Finally, someone spoke the truth of Islam that has been incoherent and distorted since 9/11.

One sign of change: the Kingdom's governmental budget for 2010 allocated SAR 500 billion for the modernization of the country—and cut SAR 1.2 billion from the budget for the Commission of Virtue and Morality officers, the mutaween.

What is the theme of Chapter 5?

To *accept* that which we are not, and *tolerate* that to which we are not accustomed, is difficult; hence, we judge to validate our self-correctness without thinking or being self-aware. What if we instead observed and questioned the unknown? Then, perhaps, we might have a full understanding of why others do what they do—which expands our acceptance and tolerance. Knowledge is infinite: If you believe you have all the answers, you are a man of no faith and no imagination.

To accept is to empathize. Empathy is the key to introspection. If you can't empathize with yourself, then how can you tolerate yourself?

CHAPTER SIX:

HOMO SAPIENS

Mazri's Law #6

The evolution of science and technology has turned *Homo sapiens* from a *thinking* species into a *feeling* species. Self-reflection, self-awareness, and self-introspection involves thinking. Lead with good thoughts.

All my life, I knew nothing but men. I grew up with them at my boys' school in Saudi Arabia. I admired their beauty, some of them, with a second look. I was always a mama's boy, sensitive and insecure. The criticism I received at an early age from my cousins made me think twice about myself, and I took it out on my siblings. Now I wish I could have been a better bigger brother. Every problem has its roots, and these roots grew so fast that I lost track of where they led me—until I was nearly six feet under.

I had no sight of female flesh nearby in Riyadh, not since my favorite cousin Safa had left for Beirut. The demons cleared the battlefield for my struggle with my sexuality. For me, it began with kissing my German cousin. He and I didn't go to second base. Just the touch of his lips and the smell of his neck made my heart beat faster with excitement, but I kept my composure. I always had an ego that played a part of its own, which soon would lead me to disaster.

He was the shy one; I always had to make the first move. Even then, I had a strong character, and I would always make sure I got what I wanted; if I didn't, depression and insecurity would set in. I was a risk-taker and a trouble-maker. (No wonder I've had such success in the corporate world.)

He had soft hair, the color of caramel, showing his German origins. My own hair is thick and dark, but I have always had a thing for softer, lighter hair. We attract what we aren't! We used to talk on the phone, each waiting for the other to say, "Come on over—Mom and the other kids have gone to shop at the mall." We used to plan sleepovers, where midnight was the most intense and erotic moment. The feeling of first romance swept us away. We didn't know much!

After three years of sinful temptation, my cousin and his family returned to Germany for good. Terrible trouble befell them—their parents separated, and their father secretly remarried in Tunisia, resulting in a baby half-sister they had never met.

When we would visit Montreal, the international city of North America, vitality was all around me. Autumn leaves would fall, snow would visit, daffodils would emerge, and summer heat would electrify Ste. Catherine Street. For the people who lived year year-round, it must have seemed mundane; but living in the land of suppression made my soul more vivacious and appreciative of every smallest thing in life.

This, I believe, is the key to genuine happiness.

While at university in Montreal, I found the search for available men a thrill. I was certainly a brave, rebellious, and adventurous young man—but lost. The fire of ambition was still there; it had never died! I turned to men-for-men chat sites to meet new singles, and went out clubbing every weekend in hopes of meeting a stud and falling in love. I was immersed in this lifestyle for four years, thinking it was the only path to true love.

My mother always knew there was something wrong with me. She would ask me directly if I was gay—which only made me feel more insecure. Was it so obvious? I wondered daily if I looked feminine. For a long time, I was afraid to tell her. I worried that she would be ashamed or embarrassed; and this in turn would make her more frustrated, as if she wanted to tell me, "I know."

I had always wanted to stand out, get attention, and be noticed. Attention fueled my ego. I was spoiled when I was a child, then felt deprived when I reached my teenage years. As a boy I had all the attention and gifts I could ever want—from my grandmother, especially—but now that my elders were a little busy, and my environment was unpleasant, I felt my lifestyle had been downgraded. I fell into depression, and sought my satisfaction elsewhere—sometimes dangerously. Wearing fashionable clothes was a way to get attention from both genders—especially men, as I had a sculptured body and knew how to show it off. I began to become proud.

During my first year studying for my degree (a Bachelor of Commerce with a major in marketing) at the John Molson School of

Business at Concordia University, I was completely focused, and earned straight A's and B's. I determined to succeed, even while my dear mother was battling breast cancer while we were all living in a duplex near my grandparents in Laval. I was angry about her illness, but my emotions were paralyzed; I was not sure what to feel. I ended up neglecting her. I had to get out and find my own pleasure and freedom from misery. I'd had enough of drama, trauma, and ill health.

But there was no escape. I would cry in the night for my dear mother. She endured so much. After her second round of chemotherapy, she hovered between life and death, too weak to walk. My father pushed her wheelchair through the corridors of Montreal's Jewish General Hospital. Her physician, Dr. Panatschi, rechecked her lab results and saw that her neutrophils were below average—a condition that could quickly turn fatal. He scowled at the nurses and ordered them to quickly take her upstairs and start her on three kinds of antibiotics to bring up her white blood cell count. If this failed, her life would be threatened.

As she looked out the window and saw the light of God shining down at her, my mother felt a sense of surrender to his will. When she awoke, there was good news; her blood counts had stabilized, and her white cells were replenishing. There would be no further chemo. She was treated with Zerodex for three years and Tamoxifen for the next five, and remains cancer-free.

In honor of my mother, I founded the Victorious Breast Cancer Foundation in Canada to support breast cancer research with an event called Victorious Time, with a celebratory fund-raiser on Mother's

Day. I had Dr. Fernand and Miss World Canada 2007 as guests of honors. I sought to partner with the Quebec Breast Cancer Foundation in return for a share of the proceeds, but they unfortunately declined to support the event. Undeterred, I sought the supports of the Canadian Breast Cancer Foundation in Toronto as well as the hospital in Montreal. I lined up globally recognized sponsors after persistent calls and follow-ups, working my way up the chain to reach the people who could help me. I refused to take "No" for an answer. My ambitious nature transformed the fear of tragedy to a more positive outlook, and that has helped me deal with the trauma. Some say I was an opportunist; at least it is better than being a pessimist! And the results speak for themselves, in the form of a sizeable donation to the hospital where my mother was treated.

We all have fears, but it is how we deal with them that matters. You can either sit with your fear and listen to the chatterbox in your mind feeding you negative thoughts, or you can be positive, get up, and start doing something constructive—preferably by extending a hand to others in your community. You are your own problem, and your own solution. My father was always against the idea of the foundation; I never understood why. But I had to do what my gut told me to. The passion just drove me further.

I ended up going back to Saudi Arabia for work, cajoled by my very persuasive father. I moved back in with him in Riyadh. This would prove economical for me, and it was a relief for my father. He simply keep me safe rather than lose me to a tempting western world; and given my lack of self-control, the job would be easier if I were under his guidance and protection. Plus, I could learn on the job and start a career as a marketing executive in his IT firm. It was a fortuitous move, forever sealing my destiny in branding. An entire career, owed to a single decision—one which at the time seemed a simple beneficial opportunity. I wonder now where I would be today if I had stayed in Montreal. For starters, I do not believe I would be writing this book.

The lack of recreation in Riyadh led me to travel often; I spent my inflated salary in London, Beirut, Dubai, and Spain. It was an opportunity to see the world—and to better understand myself. Traveling helped me see a world where I could think for myself and define my own passion, interests, and identity in a free world.

One weekend, I made a brief escape to the design and fashion capital of the Middle East, Beirut. The city is situated on a landmass at the midpoint of Lebanon's Mediterranean coast. Beirut, alongside the rest of Lebanon, was put under the French Mandate after the First World War. Lebanon became independent in 1943, and took Beirut as its capital city. The city remained a local scholarly capital, turning into a noteworthy tourist destination and a banking haven, particularly during the Persian Gulf oil boom. This period of relative thriving ended in 1975 when civil war broke out. During the conflict, Beirut was segregated between the Muslim west part and the Christian east coast, and Syrian troops began a partial occupation that would continue for three decades. Since to the end of the war in 1990, the city has been largely rebuilt, and by the beginning of the 2006 Israel–Lebanon conflict, the city had to some degree recovered its status as the social and scholarly heart of the Middle East and as the center for business, design, tourism, and media. The reconstruction of downtown Beirut has been to a great extent driven by Solidere, a development organization founded in 1994 by Lebanese Prime Minister Rafik Hariri, who was tragically killed by a car bomb in 2005. His death set off a series of peaceful protests that resulted in the establishment of an independent Lebanon, free from Syrian occupation.

Beirut is a known haven for nightlife. Clubs and pubs sprawl along Monoe and Gymayzie Streets. It has also a getaway for gay men to party, mingle, and satisfy their deepest desires. When I visited, I found the men (and the women) to be stunning, almost without exception—despite their pompous attitudes that will get them nowhere—especially the metrosexual men. In general, the gay community in Beirut is friendly, loving, fashionable, social, and full of life. Lebanon is the only country in the Middle East that advocates awareness for HIV/AIDS, and is home to Helem, the first Arab LGBTQ rights organization powered by a legitimate non-governmental non-profit foundation (registered in Quebec, surprisingly enough).

According to the perspective of western media, gay rights activism in the Arab world is nonexistent. It is impossible to fly the rainbow flag when homosexual acts are criminalized in all but three of the twenty-two countries of the Arab world, and are punishable by death in Yemen, Iraq, Qatar, Saudi Arabia, Somalia, Sudan, and the UAE. Yet despite article 534 of the Lebanese penal code—which criminalizes "sexual intercourse contrary to the laws of nature"—Beirut has become the most liberal city in the Arab world for LGBTQ rights.

Today, 33 million people worldwide live with HIV, of whom only

8 million are in treatment. I am lucky to be a Canadian citizen who has access to medical care. My diabetes has proved to be much more troublesome to deal with than HIV. Living with HIV is not associated with physical pain or daily injection of insulin in the abdomen. Some people do not even know they have it. If you are sexually active, I strongly advise STD testing every three to six months at least. Never take your own life for granted, even if HIV is now no longer a death sentence. It is not worth it to trade your life for fifteen minutes of sexual intercourse.

Without your health, how can you even work and earn an income? With good health, you can accomplish your dreams. God had blessed me, and for too long I took that for granted. Every illness is manmade, I believe. Our health has so much to do with what we eat, what we do, how we breathe, where we live, and the lifestyle we lead. We think we have it all figured out, but we don't. We think an illness won't strike us, but who are you to say you are an exception? You are a *Homo sapiens* like everybody else. You are not that special, so be humble; don't be so narcissistic that you exempt yourself from the world's misery and wonders. We only consider ourselves as belonging to this world if it has wonders to give us; if it brings negativity to our life, we resent it. We convince ourselves that the worst can't happen to us, even as we fear for our children's lives, telling them to be careful and not take risks at school. Those children grow up fearing every obstacle life brings them; when circumstances dissolve their dreams or tarnish their accomplishments, they can't handle it. But every misery makes us stronger. Every hardship makes our skin thicker. Every experience is a journey from which to learn. Every risk taken generates higher profits. Every fear crushed means we something new we can accomplish in this world. Thank you to all the "fearless" scientists who every day overcome their fears of seeing deaths happen before their eyes, and instead use that energy to develop new medications. What about the soldiers that fear dying, but face their fears anyway to fight for their country? What about the children diagnosed with cancer who still laugh and play daily, defying their illness?

Just because the world identifies HIV as a taboo doesn't mean we must live according to that branding. The simple fact of a medical diagnosis can mean being stereotyped by people who have serophobia—a manifestation of fear directed toward HIV-positive people. Serophobia is expressed in actions like excluding HIV-positive people from communities, unjust and unnecessary distancing or discontinuation of visits, gossiping about someone's HIV sero-status, or revealing confidential information. Discrimination is often associated with the illness, and organizations such as www.stopserophobia.com (based in Montreal) are on a mission to end this callous bigotry against HIV-positive people. Everything that the Arab countries were against, I challenged it.

As soon as I landed back in Riyadh, my chatterbox went into overdrive, the demons filling my head with negative thoughts: *You are bound to die. You are worthless. You have nothing anymore; no one will love you, your dreams are shattered. You will only be pitied. You wanted out of Saudi Arabia? Now your wish will be my command.*

My fear of death increased, and so did my fear of challenges. I became overcautious. My sense of adventure began to decline.

What brought me back was reading the book *Feel the Fear and Do It Anyway*, by Susan Jeffers. The lessons of this book made me think wisely about life. I learned to take responsibility for my own illness, knowing that it was man-made, as God is Good. The Quran confirms this, that all illnesses and treatments are man-made; God brings forth the good, which could be the scientific minds found in our world or the miracles of healing that still exist. We have forever heard of cancer patients being healed by positive thinking. They must give all their problems and worries to God, we are told, and he will have his way with them. A higher power is something that we can't control, but we can learn from our pain.

Jeffers's book also advises us to accept any illness or problem, along with the associated pain, and simply "do it anyway"—do what we have in our hearts to do, counteracting the fear within ourselves with a recognition that the chatterbox talking down to us is not right.

Most of the time, when it tells you that you are not healthy, or that you are dying, or that you're not smart, you can counter that negativity with a simple thought: *I am standing, I am breathing, and I can solve the simplest mathematics problem with incredible ease: $2 \times 2 = 4$.*

I remind myself, "I am normal and healthy" almost thirty times every day. In the Quran, it says throw all your worries to God to be sorted: *Inchallah.*

Inchallah is a word often used in the Islamic religion to mean "God willing," or "If God wills it"—a powerful affirmation that gives us hope. *Inchallah* I will get through this successfully. *Inchallah* I will be destined for success and fortune. Religion is not a restriction on our ambitions—and if it is, it is definitely for our own good. I have learned that God did not put his creations in this world to suffer, as suffering is manmade. God wants us to realize the truth in this world and live happily with a purpose. The agony of fear associated with my illness has taught me to spread love and open my arms as a daily exercise, to invite into my life whatever God sends me. The more we are welcoming to what God has destined for us, the more positivity we invite, leaving God to handle our greatest problems.

In Islam, we learn that when we are faced with an illness, it is because God loves us and has chosen us. Yes, chosen you! He wants to balance your sins against your positive deeds; whenever you are hurt and call out to God for help, God starts washing out your sins. God deserves recognition for all the blessings he has given us, even the smallest of them—hearing, sight, even the ability to put bread on the table when (according to the US Census Bureau) approximately 46 million people in the USA alone live have an annual income of less than $23,000 for a family of four.

We tend to look at our problems and flaws rather than our blessings. But in the end, we all die with nothing in our hands or pockets. We will not be taking with us the one million dollars in our HSBC bank account, or our iPhone 5G. So live happy and righteously doing what you want to do. Find your true calling by simply listening to the signs around you—those whispers that give you second thoughts. Follow the truth; learn to accept it; and don't be afraid of change.

I have come to understand my own deepest insecurities—the fears that led me to the devil in disguise. My promiscuous behavior, my romantic fantasies, were a reaction against suppression. I wanted to be in the arms of people and be loved because of the inner void, the feeling of being starved for affection in an oppressed country. I wanted to feel secure, loved, cared for. I wanted to tell the world, "Look at me! I am here! Do you see me?"

Oh yes, they saw me—as a sex object. Which was exactly how I wanted to be seen. I thought that was the only solution. I thought it would validate me. Through seduction, I thought I could lure people in and hope that they would see the real me. Unfortunately, I lured the wrong people in the wrong way, falling onto the wrong path.

To achieve what is right for us in life, we must learn to think right, live right, and be right in our minds. The more energy you give, the more you will get back. But be careful what kind of energy you are putting out around you. Take responsibility for the energy you give out, wherever you go. All I know is that what has been done to me has already been done to my enemies—if any, as my nature is not to dislike.

What is the theme of Chapter 6?

Since Adam and Eve, human beings have been self-expressive. The relationships among the children of Adam proved acceptable at the time because *norms* are relative to time—but not vice-versa. Seeking love in different ways is tied to freedom of expression, creating unity and a sharing society, rather than a divided nation spreading hatred for future generations to acquire.

Let your faith guide you to your true self.

CHAPTER SEVEN:

BRAND CULTURE

Mazri's Law #7

**We live in a cluttered digital world made of
brands—people, products, and places.
If you fail to communicate your strengths
boldly, then you will fail to be the next
ordinary leader in today's unordinary era.**

My internal conflicts and hardships have never stood in the way of my ambitions, and I've devoted hard work to my dreams of becoming a true success in the corporate world of today's globalized digital economy. Since the age of three, I have been addicted to commercials. My father used to record hours of commercials on VHS tapes, and I would watch them hour after hour.

I was fascinated by jingles at this young age. The older I grew, the more intrigued I was by the amount of creative content that could be packed into only thirty seconds to communicate a strong, emotional marketing message or story.

I always felt I had a message to tell the world, and when I was sixteen years old I started a young men's magazine that circulated among my peers at my private school. My little publishing project discussed issues about gadgets, success, self-help, girls, and business—topics that I wrote about all by myself. I worked until 3:00 AM on weekdays and weekends. It was a great way to pass the time in a place where I had little choice but to sit at home and make use of my talents in the best way I could find.

I founded Victorious Breast Cancer Foundation in 2007, at age twenty, inspired by my mother's diagnosis in the fall of 2005. I registered as a non-profit foundation in Quebec and created the benefit gala event called Victorious Time in Montreal city. The event generated media frenzy and attention from Montreal hospitals interested in raising funds for their own breast cancer initiatives. The red carpet event was an emotional roller coaster for my mother and me, especially when I welcomed her on stage with open arms to discuss her recovery in front of 200 VIP guests. We ended up raising more than $100,000 at our inaugural Mother's Day event.

I had successfully branded the event by creating three brand mascots—superheroines called "Victorious Women," dressed in custom-made costumes. These characters featured in outdoor advertisements, metro billboard ads, newspapers, Global Canada TV, and major-market radio.

Victorious was a provincial campaign, channeling my sorrow and anger toward positive change, celebrating all the victorious women across Quebec. This was my first branding case study, one that has enabled me to look deeper and discover my true genuine talent—storytelling and branding. I believe we are all walking brands, with our own unique story according to our individual position in society. I see branding possibilities in products, places, and people. All have a distinct message, if you listen carefully. There is no brand without a listening audience!

I wouldn't stop there. When I turned twenty-one, I founded a boutique branding company from my parent's basement in Laval, working on small jobs—banners, flyers, and local SME marketing projects. My most important early project was building my own agency's brand. AB Communications was started from the ground up, all the way from the West to the Middle East; I partnered with a modern Saudi patriot whose family had become famous for water drilling in the Kingdom since 1953. The young sheikh was a positive, ambitious, diplomatic, and caring gentleman, a family man who shared my vision: to brand the country, starting with the local bakeries and gas stations, with their dirty banners and ill-matched logos. Here was a Saudi man to look up, a role model for every young ambitious man with dreams of success. He was a real Muslim in heart and mind, teaching me not just how to conduct business and negotiate in the Middle East—a task at which so many American companies have failed because of their disregard for cultural marketing and communication— but he also taught me about the stigma faced by Islam's brand in the western media. It may sound flippant to speak of a major world religion as facing a branding problem, but it's true. There is a widespread misperception of Islam's doctrines by the west, obscuring the truth of its origins and practices as a religion of peace, empathy, and tolerance.

AB Communications' mission is to creatively address the external communication gaps present in the world of commerce today. We are all about crafting the brand image from the inside out. This boutique branding firm aims to be recognized as *brand image enhancers* by specializing in building up brand personalities, retelling creative stories, generating a flow of new ideas, and developing advertising that lives up to the hype. Sometimes we like to refer to ourselves as "brand groomers," equipped with a unique process called *Brandment* that assists in enhancing and better defining your brand's personality, resulting in creativity-effectiveness.

In the AB corporate profile, you would find quotes that express my philosophy of branding:

To understand advertising is to understand branding. We discover your brand's unique voice, build your brand personality, and tell you a brand story.

We think, breathe, feel, and live the brand with creative attitude.

Advertising, the world's most powerful art form, is about propelling products out into the marketplace and maintaining the flow of the economy. Branding, by contrast, is about corporate power, which needs to be nurtured by advertising. Acquiring corporate power begins with a B2C communications problem, making it a B2B communications challenge.

AB Communications believes that clients must offer consumers not commodities, but a lifestyle—an experience that will make them feel. This process is called branding, and fosters the creation of a brand culture—a set of values, ideas, and attributes. It is remarkable how branding can add asset-value to a corporation! Al Ries, the godfather of branding positioning, was my mentor; he founded the study of brand positioning, or occupying a single category as the leading brand in the subconscious minds of consumers.

My career made me a constant presence on TV and radio, and in national newspapers and periodical magazines by the age of twenty-five. I have branded myself as the brand guru of Saudi Arabia. I've capitalized on my understanding of the gap in branding that existed in the country. I thought that I could fill the void before somebody else did. That's where I was wrong. Many have tried, but the cultural attitude could not be changed. Saudi clients wanted what they wanted, notwithstanding the logic behind the creative execution of a branding strategy. That made Saudi Arabia was a unique market, where I had to learn sour patience and tolerance!

By late 2012, I understood that the only way for the corporate culture to start think of brand equity as an intangible asset in their balance sheet—and as a unique selling proposition to lend a competitive edge in this global digital economy—was to educate and develop the culture, and fast. I also found a gap in branding education and researched more about then-King Abdullah's vision of achieving a diversified economy more founded on non-oil sector businesses, which at the time accounted for only 10 percent of the Kingdom's GDP. This opened doors to discuss the keys of competitive advantage for non-oil products such as consumer packaged goods, diary, electronics, and other products produced locally.

The answer to unlocking King Abdullah's vision was nothing else than branding local products against international products imported from Europe and North America. But how can one compete against giant brands such as La Vache Qui Rit, Nutella, or Kellogg's? I realized the importance of organizing an event and seminar in Saudi Arabia to create branding awareness and shed some light on the benefits of branding vs. advertising. I leveraged my deep insights about the market trends, consumer behavior, purchasing patterns, and emotional responsiveness to brands. The key to true success is believing that there is no one and nothing that can hold you back—believing in positive change and in your own capabilities, knowing that you can accomplish your dreams. little by little, with patience and persistence; there is nothing you can achieve over a single day and night. However, to make success more attainable, you must link your capabilities, aptitudes, passion, and desire to succeed and couple them with introspection—examination of one's own thoughts, self-awareness, and perceptions—in the present state.

There are those who will be busy socializing, drinking, dancing, and gossiping, along with others who decline dinners, parties and social events in order to focus on the vision in front of them, to bring it to completion without interruption or distraction. It's not a question of wrong or right, simply a choice. But successful people understand the power of utter focus. Focus and you shall attain! Let nothing distract you from your vision. Know that you can remake yourself; you can make a new blueprint for your subconscious mind, cultivating a more positive attitude. Always rejoice in the success and good fortune of others; this will attract good fortune for yourself. Always try to know everything about one thing, not everything about everything. Specialize in your own field. Do it differently from others; be unusual. Successful people are not selfish, but simply want to serve humanity and society through quality service. Feed your conscious mind with images of success; picture yourself attaining your desires, and this will feed your subconscious mind and manifest in positive energy.

There is nothing more powerful than acquiring a positive subconscious mindset. I have forever been ravaged, leading me to maintain a negative mindset, holding nothing but grudges, fear, sorrow, distress, and tension in my body and mind. This has obviously caused hardships in my life, including illnesses that have manifested from my mental pictures and thoughts. You are what you think. Be careful what you think of, not what you wish for. You are your only failure or success. There is only you to blame for your life—not your mother, father, or high school teacher. Change is around the corner and you must focus on the present—which also means "gift"—and not the past, which is history, or the future, which is unknown.

I have learned to apply positive affirmations, repeating them every morning when I wake and every night before I sleep, which is when the subconscious mind is quiet and processing all the data from your conscious mind. I repeat to myself, *I am successful; I am strong; I am fearless; I am healthy; I am wealthy; I am peaceful; I am forgiving;* and *I am loving.* These affirmations have strongly manifested in my life, attracting nothing but positive energy. We are all energy; people receive and give whatever energy is available in the room. Take responsibility for the energy you give to others. Remember: the more you give, the more you get back. Therefore, think twice what you give!

When we talk about success, we use money as a measurement. Wealth is not a taboo, although it sometimes holds a negative connotation. Perhaps your grandmother has said to you—and grandmothers everywhere have always said—"Son, money is dirt in your hands. It is only meant to be spent. Don't hold on to it." What she meant, of course, is that we should not be selfish and hoard wealth; but too many people nowadays feel guilty about money, or undeserving of wealth at all—and that is not the true key of happiness. Yes, happiness is a state of mind, but there is absolutely no punishment in wishing for wealth in your short life and working to attain security.

Many think they don't deserve it, but you must know that everyone deserves wealth—and all other good things. You are deserving of the riches of health, love, and fortune. Never think otherwise; those negative thoughts that you engrave in your subconscious mind will manifest in your life. All we need can be summed up in the L-words— Life and Love. We can't live without the L-word. (And no, it doesn't stand for "Lesbian" only!)

What is the theme of Chapter 7?

We often feel guilty about accepting wealth in a given society. We incriminate ourselves for accumulating fortunes in life, because of our misconceptions or ideologies associated with money. We associate wealth with arrogance and immorality. We feel undeserving.

Learn to empathize with yourself, to afford yourself greater compassion. Know that you are deserving of the greatest riches and the fullest happiness in life, without remorse. Money is not shameful, as our ancestors taught us: rather, it brings new opportunities, encouraging you to give a hand to those in need and create a prosperous life for yourself and your community. The keys to wealth are ambition, determination, and acquisition of unique skills, such as branding yourself. People buy into the man behind the brand, not the product. Think and control every impulse within your mind to achieve self-mastery.

Rebrand, rethink, relive!

CHAPTER EIGHT:

LOVE IS EASY

Mazri's Law #8

We are born independently and will die indecently. Learn to love and cherish yourself before learning to fall in love with others. Love is there for you; start being there for yourself.

I was loved and indulged with affection in my childhood by my mother and grandmother, but grew up to become deprived of intimacy and love. Solitude took over my life, isolating me in my black and white room, as my father became both preoccupied and overdemanding. The love of a man was an absolute need for me, but my father failed to understand what lay beneath my egotistical shell—that he was needed.

My first love was called *Canada*. I was narrow-minded, thinking that any country must look like Canada or the United States; and if it didn't, it failed to satisfy me.

I appreciated the concrete houses with basements, and the wooden parquet floors. I also appreciated humane spirit of the neighborhoods, the stop signs that said "Arrêt," the sidewalks that motivated people to walk freely, and the bike track from uptown to downtown Montreal. Everything about Canada lived in my mind, and nothing would measure up to her standards.

I realized that love for something or someone must grow with time as you become habituated, developing a deep level of understanding for the other partner, place, or thing. So if someone tells you they love you after the first date, run away! You also develop a sense of attachment that would be hard to simply break overnight. Love can grow, even if it starts with hatred; you just simply have to sacrifice and hang in there, if you desire to do so, and trust that the rewards are greater than the risk. Sometimes we are not aware of the destination, but we must learn to embrace the journey; love can only grow within us is when we learn from every negative experience and cultivate a positive outlook with patience, tolerance, and perseverance. Nothing comes easy; that's just the way it is!

I expressed my mingled love and resentment toward Saudi Arabia in a poem I wrote as I sat at my round white table in my black-and-white checkered room, under the window overlooking a tall white wall isolating every villa and neighbor from the other, with a view of the satellite dishes and water tank on the neighbor's roof. What an inspiring vista, indeed; it disgusts me!

Dear Saudi Arabia,

I write to you and only you,
To express my love and anger for you.
You have given me shelter,

You have nurtured me forever,

You have watched over my pitfalls and success

Knowing I have gone through a mess

Trying to find myself

In the middle of the desert

Where love is impossible

Until you made me realize the only love I need

Is the love within which I must breed.

Saudi Arabia, you have taught me to love myself

After consecutive heartbreaks in your sandy land

Where on my head I would always land

But you brought me back up with your wisdom and love

That for long I have taken for granted

Blaming you for all my pain

And failing to see what I'd gained.

Saudi Arabia, you never lost hope for me

As you knew very well what you have raised.

I traveled the world and the seven seas and lost myself

To find myself in your land again.

Yes, you possess your suppressive rules

Yes, you know no freedom

Yes, you are intolerant to sins

Yes, you imprison the adventurous souls

And yes, you claim to know no evil

But may I kindly say that you unknowingly created devils in your
land

What was once an angel in Heaven became a devil in Hell.

You have forced your laws onto your citizens

In the process creating little monsters among us

Which was never your intention

Saudi Arabia, I write to you and only you,

To express my love and hate for you.

I will always love you

No matter the worst have experienced

Which nevertheless

Has brought the best out of me. I love you as I have grown

Wiser, faster

Stronger, louder, Peaceful and collected...

Thank you, Saudi Arabia, for loving me.

* * *

Back at work in the Kingdom, I still faced monotony. But I made great friends along the way, who have filled my life with joy and laughter. My two best friends were supportive, loving, mature, and wise; they loved my character and personality that filled the room with joy and life. I felt that they were all I had outside the Mazri family, and I developed a particular attachment to them over time. I was younger than both of them by an average of five years. With time, I had come to understand that I was very needy, and rude when angry. I tended to take people and things for granted, and never realized their value; I was ungrateful for what I had, and inundated with thoughts of what I didn't.

I have always been focused on finding the love that will grant me warmth, intimacy, acceptance, and validation. I knew that it would be hard to find love in Saudi Arabia—a land where angels become demons in the face of oppression that has killed people's temptations, desires, and human needs. It was a hopeless place indeed!

I knew that if I were to have a dating life, it would have to be outside of the country. I had the means to travel to the neighboring countries almost every weekend. The only way forward for anything lasting would be a long-distance relationship. At this point, though, I was indifferent as to whether it was long or short distance; I simply knew that I needed just a little bit of love and attention, and I was prepared to do whatever it took to jump on the next joyride of love.

I was always fixated on receiving love, and did not comprehend that relationships in life are all about giving. It is simply a reciprocal relationship rule. I was obviously a novice with relationships, and showed little compassion or respect for what my partners wanted or desired. It was a relationship with myself that I desired with other partners as it was a "Me" Relationship. I was affection-deprived and lived in an environment that had affected my personality, behavior, and mental health on many levels—especially my social and personal lives.

Sometimes, I wondered why I sacrificed every day to settle in a country that imprisoned my wants and desires. Was it my destiny? Was it the voice within that told me, "Don't leave yet! Something great will come your way." I Saudi Arabia, I had at least achieved financial stability; was this an omen? Was the experience and career that I enjoyed at this young age a sign? Was it worth throwing all these fascinating accomplishments away for a little bit of love and intimacy, and perhaps some validation on the side? I was a rebel and a dream-follower; I knew better, I thought, than to subdue my ambitions and sacrifice my life for a salary at the end of the month. I truly believe there was a voice within speaking to me and telling me to hang in there. The light will appear only in the darkness. But why should I decide to stay in the dark when I could have the light any time I wanted?

Nevertheless, my journey in Saudi Arabia was an emotional fluctuation, a time of living on the edge, filled with impatience. The environment turned me into a cat on a hot tin roof; I was filled with yearning for romance. I had a deep attachment to the idea of love—but not yet the actual determination to really love. I had not yet learned that attachment is the root of all unhappiness. Attaching oneself to something or someone can create mental trauma, unless one proceeds from an understanding that this love or desire can be lost, forgotten, or reduced over time without affecting one's own state of happiness. To attach yourself to a particular desire fulfills your egocentric need to feel validated or important, but it's a temporary fix, arising from the deep insecurities. What's missing is the simplicity of reinforcing to yourself that your self is all you need.

I never truly loved myself, because genuine love is found on the inside, and to truly love we must do so freely—including accepting our insecurities. I recognized my father's voice in the back of my head: "Love is care, and if you truly love someone then you must learn to respect their decisions, let them go, and wish them the best. Forgive them for whatever hurts they have caused you. Show nothing but gratitude for the lessons you have learned from them—lessons you can apply in your next relationship, the one that may last a lifetime. That is true love, son! Love is neither possessive nor strategic. It is the action from the heart on a journey to eternity."

I regret not having learned this earlier. For far too long, I tended to push people to love me more, always demanding *more* from my partners—more text messages, more calls, more reassurances. Being needy will push a partner away; we are rushing them to adapt to our expectations and our routines—and no one routine works for everyone.

We all have different expectations, perceptions, and ideas about a relationship, and they can be very different between two parties. But only time can reveal such differences. And only by taking time can we come to a mutual understanding and meet each other halfway, if both are willing to sacrifice.

I never understood the meaning of taking things slow. I am an Aries, after all, and as a fire sign my personality tends to be engaged in achieving, in living fast and acting without delay. Life is short. Living every moment is like trying to catch one's breath. Time is valuable and must not be taken for granted. We Aries are usually very expressive and run faster than the rest of the zodiac signs. We are always ahead emotionally, as we tend to be very introspective and introverted, working on ourselves and analyzing, dissecting, and interpreting the details of every situation we have experienced to attain valuable insights, always looking for new wisdom that will forever change us for the better. And we are able to perform such tasks at a very fast pace and in a very short time period.

Over time, I understood the importance of respecting other people's values and wants. Everyone has different perceptions about life, relationships, and success—but we tend to assume that everyone thinks the same way we do, or even that our way of thinking is objectively right. But it's narcissistic and ignorant to regard other people's attitudes and thinking as homogeneous. Living in the digital world today, I always thought that a few WhatsApp messages or a Viber phone call could maintain the momentum of a relationship—enough to stay connected, enough to make the other person feel we belong together. However, such mechanisms do not resonate easily with some people, especially independent and individualistic personalities. Such people find it hard to resort to social media or digital communication for hours, but may make an effort to respect your wishes. And we must do the same in return: to attempt to understand and respect them. The number of text messages you send does not equate to the love you have for the other; rather, it is the thought of always coming back and communicating with your partner, keeping up with their day-to-day activities just because you care for them. Sometimes, it is hard work to maintain the momentum of a relationship. We expect a message on Facebook, a few text messages on WhatsApp messenger, maybe a phone call or a few likes on our Instagram. We have to be much more introspective in this digital era!

It's funny how our attitudes and perceptions have changed with the advent of the digital age. Our expectations are rising sky-high while our disappointments are through the floor. A few missed messages on social media can leave us feeling neglected, with a sense of invalidation, insignificance, and unhappiness. We as human beings tend to set benchmarks and KPI (key performance indicators) in our lives to measure the outcome of our relationships, careers, and even friendships. It is no longer about the journey, or about doing things freely with love and compassion without any expectation of return. Rather, we're loaded up with daily tasks that don't come from the heart. We push people to feel a certain way and act accordingly, making them feel pressured; and what was once a relationship will turn to no more than acquaintanceship, at best, as they don't want to feel the coercion.

This also holds true for marriages. Oprah Winfrey explained in an interview with Barbra Walters how marriage infuses expectations for both partners to meet where love has become secondary. Rather than being the top priority—feeling love and actualizing it on a daily basis—it takes a backseat. We know that to achieve an optimal relationship we've got to show more compassion, love, care, and passion to each other on a daily basis. This entails eradicating our expectations for what is given or merely routine, and working to achieve the desired kind of love by giving every day, enhancing the journey for one another—focusing not on the destination, it's about the journey.

On New Year's Day, 2014, I landed at London's Stansted airport. A minicab driver was waiting for me in arrivals, holding a white card with my name on it. Under a gloomy sky, as he drove me to Heathrow for my connecting flight to Montreal, I started chatting with the driver, asking him about Prince William and Kate. What do the people think of them in London, I wondered, given that they are always under the spotlight—especially with their then-newborn baby.

"Oh, they are just fabulous," the driver said. "But you know, since Diana's death, nothing has been the same. The people don't trust the

Crown like they used to. Not since they planned her death."

"Please, I said, "do tell me more."

"You will be shocked," the driver responded. "Are you ready?"

I told him I was, and he told the whole story. Princess Diana, as he described her, was young, naïve, a good-hearted woman teaching in a kindergarten before she was thrown to the wolves. Prince Charles's grandmother knew Diana's grandmother, and both had arranged to introduce her to Charles after he came back from the military.

Charles never loved Diana; he was already in love with Camilla, and they were planning to get engaged until he left for the military. He would be gone for six years, some promise of engagement, so naturally Camilla sought for some kind of validation of commitment. Prince Charles felt it wasn't the right time, and told her that he couldn't commit. And so Camilla told him she couldn't wait forever without some kind of confirmation of his love for her.

Well, Prince Charles began his military service and soon afterward Camilla married a respectable military officer and had two children. The driver shook his head. "Prince Charles sure did regret it," he said, "but he had to move on."

Charles met Diana through his grandmother, just as planned, and married her. Camilla, in the meantime, divorced her husband. Charles had occasion for repentance, but what he really wanted at this point was a male heir. And for that purpose, Diana was the perfect victim.

"Diana loved Charles, she truly did," said the driver. "All she ever wanted was a romantic love life, swept away like rose petals, gone with the wind through the garden. All an illusion, you see."

Because while romance remained a top priority for Diana, her relationship with Charles began to suffer; he began seeing Camilla behind her back. The jealous Diana couldn't live in a love triangle; she still dreamed of some Prince Charming who would sweep her off her feet, but all she had was an unfaithful Prince of Wales.

One day at Windsor, at the Cartier Polo Championship, Princess Diana was the guest of honor and presented a trophy to the charming, masculine, and seductive Major James Hewitt. Hewitt was an independent playboy who was smitten by Diana's glamour, poise, and beauty as she presented him with the trophy.

"You can Google 'Hewitt and Diana'," said the driver. "Look at that photo of when she was presenting him with the trophy. Doesn't he remind you of someone? Why, he's the absolute twin of—are you ready?—Prince Harry!"

I was shocked. "Go on," I said eagerly.

"Well, the Queen was not happy, as you can well imagine," said the driver. " She saw Diana as a risk and a threat. Top promiscuous for a proper royal. And Diana's attitude didn't sit well with her."

Charles and Diana separated, allowing Charles to be with Camilla, but Diana was still on her path of discovery—still searching for true love. She began feeling the void and loneliness. She was always under the scrutiny of the royal family, even when she was living alone. Diana dated James Hewitt for a year, till he also took advantage of her loving heart. "They called him a playboy, and that's just what he was," said the driver. "Playing with that poor girl's heart."

Diana was left heartbroken, depressed, and lonely. Finally letting go of the illusion of love with Hewitt, Diana fell in love with a renowned Indian surgeon—this before her affair with Dodi Fayed and ultimately her death.

"Rumor has it that the royal family arranged the whole thing," said the driver. "She was pregnant with Dodi's baby, they say. Imagine! A Muslim Englishman somewhere in line for the throne! That's the last thing the Crown needed in this modern time. So it was a done thing. Only it didn't quite as planned. The driver and Dodi died instantly, but not the bodyguard, who made it out alive—and not Diana, who was alive after the crash. The ambulance rushed her to a hospital 100 kilometers away instead of one nearby, and then they wrapped her body like a mummy. Why? No one ever knew the reason."

Hearing this story—a tale of romance gone wrong, of lives destroyed by the illusion of love—filled me with appreciation and gratitude; a chance encounter with a cab driver had opened my eyes. I began to develop an enlightened perception of love. I understood that one must always feel the joy of one's own company, learning to love oneself and feeding the subconscious mind daily with this simple truth: "I am all I need, and I am sufficient."

I knew in that instant that love is a lengthy process, similar to making the finest wine. As love matures, its finest flavors emerge. The longer it lasts, the more lovely it is to drink. Love can't be pushed, cajoled, or rushed. It is a deep emotion; every person experiences it differently, and we can't expect anyone else to react as we believe they should according to some stereotyped depiction of love. We all show love in our own unique colors. It is only when we look into these details, understand, appreciate, and give back love that the universe will assist in manifesting nothing but love in return.

Diana died broken-hearted, and was never truly loved because she never believed that she would be loved. On a daily basis, she had fed her mind with negative thoughts, delving deep into loneliness, emptiness, and lack of fulfilment. She focused on what she lacked rather than looking at what she had. If you give praise and gratitude for your blessings, the universe itself will plot in your favor. But she was impatient and needy, and these two attributes are destructive to the soul.

I very much related to Princess Diana's story, as I always had a need to be loved intimately. I too craved the illusion of living a Romeo-and-Juliet romantic fairy tale. Like Diana, I failed to love myself—to recognize my strengths and work to overcome my weaknesses so as to live a fruitful life, wiser and free of major flaws that might threaten any relationship. I failed to prepare myself for solitude, and complained regularly about it.

Author Paulo Coelho writes that in solitude, we will understand and respect the love that has left us and decide whether it is worth asking that love to come back or if we should simply let go and embark on a new path. The divine energy responds best when we are still and silent; solitude is a blessing, for it is the only time when the light illuminates everything around us and helps us to see more clearly. It makes an immense difference to the quality of our work when it's underscored by silent reflection.

Coelho describes how the artist's talent shines, and how the work is at its best, when the artist is alone, still, and silent. Do not fear solitude;

do not be afraid of your own company; do not go desperately looking to amuse yourself and keep yourself busy to avoid being alone. It is only in solitude when our soul speaks to us and helps us decide what to do with our life.

I first encountered Paulo Coelho's work when an Australian acquaintance living in Dubai gave me a copy of his bestselling novel *The Alchemist*. That in turn led me to discover another of his books, *The Manuscript Found in Accra*. This book enlarged my paradigm of thinking and changed my perceptions of love and success. Reading it, I realized that being a true lover does not mean co-dependence. Love does not depend on spending every hour by my side, or connecting with me on WhatsApp nine hours a day, or liking my pictures on Facebook. Our digital lifestyle has given us unreasonable expectations in terms of friendships and relationships; but the true lover realizes that love is loyalty, and loyalty goes hand in hand with freedom. When we truly love, Coelho tells us, we do so without mistrust, disloyalty, or the fear of betrayal.

I had worked for four years in Saudi Arabia—not to mention seven years of high school—and spent my every last penny overseas to take in life, visiting different countries and different cultures before returning again to my tedious routine in Saudi Arabia. I grew bored, and asked myself if this was all that God had planned out for me: a job from 9:00 AM to 5:00 PM every day, in a place where I couldn't enjoy cinemas, clubs, bars, lounges, or even just a lively walk among men and women. My father always seemed content for me to have a steady decent job, but I was restless. I knew there was something else out there that would satisfy me and fill me with joy. There had to be something to give me a reason to live. I traveled around the world and back again to the middle of nowhere, and I was unhappy; not necessarily with the lifestyle in Saudi Arabia, as I had accustomed myself to its bizarre lifestyle—but something deeper was missing. There was a call that I couldn't quite hear. I was trying to listen. If only everyone would be quiet—the voices in my head, my father, my friends, my mother, I mean *everyone*—so that I could listen to this subtle voice. Because this time, I would do anything in my power to change my life *now*.

What is the theme of Chapter 8?

Life is self-discovery; habit is a self-constraint. Adapting to something or someone for too long results in a magnetic attachment, yielding to a sense of loss if we lose it. We must learn the competency of detachment instead; we are born alone and die alone.

Attach with compassion, care, and love, but don't create a habit of closeness.

Your ultimate solution is to embrace solitude through traveling or temporary retreats. This is how you achieve self-mastery. Be introverted; understand why you feel what you feel. You will realize most of your emotions were a result of some habit. Break it before it breaks you!

CHAPTER NINE:

HOLLYWOOD'S CALLING

Mazri's Law #9

Every human lives on the 7 F's:

*Fame, Fortune, F*cking, Friends, Family, Farts, and Food.*

Actor, director, doctor, or housekeeper—they are all the same. Don't let them fool you.

When I was six years old, back in Montreal, I would come home from school, drop my school bag, and wash my hands before lunch. My mother would come to the lavatory, hide her hands behind her back, and ask me to choose a hand. I always would get it right, somehow; when she took her hand from behind her back, she'd be holding a VHS tape of the latest Walt Disney—*Tarzan, Toy Story*, and many more. Soon I had the entire Disney collection in their white plastic VHS covers. Movies let me to escape to my wildest and most exhilarating imagination, a place where worries, fear, and insecurities did not exist. If I had one dream in my childhood, it was to become an actor.

My brother, sister, and I would play Power Rangers in the basement of our home (I was always the Red Ranger). Batman was another favorite; I would tie my blanket around my neck like his black cape, and jump from one sofa to another. I loved playing everyone and anyone but myself. It was an escape, and salvation for my soul. I found utter satisfaction in performing.

As I grew older, I came to understand that America—specifically Hollywood—was the home of the movies and cartoons I loved. America was the land of dreams and hope, where you can be whoever you wanted to be: the land of opportunities, where hard work is rewarded and success is pervasive. Canadian like myself, of course, would need a green card to legally work there; I never understood such procedures. I was ignorant and careless, as I always knew that I would go where my family would go. For a while, my father had tried to move to Los Angeles, the city of angels, a place he had fallen in love with; but whatever he had planned did not work according to his expectations. Montreal was our home, and it was the only city that was good to us—despite having the highest taxes in North America. The community service, healthcare and education were unsurpassed, making this a country to envy. Americans still marry Canadians to get better healthcare. I never understood arranged marriages.; in any case, I never thought I would ever have to encounter such situations.

My father always said "No" to whatever I wanted during my adolescence. I always wanted to enter theatre and graduate in fine arts;

but like a typical Arab, he viewed such fields with disdain, as shameful pursuits that put no bread and butter on the table. Perhaps he was right: but what if that was the only field that gave me a purpose to live and wake up early with a smile on my face?

That was of no concern to my father; he wanted me to become a lawyer. When I finally left the Arab world, moving back to Canada for university, I studied marketing with a minor in economics. I was a straight-A student, but I felt like a robot: waking up daily, doing what I must do—doing what was asked of me by society. I felt I had no voice; I was trapped in a field that I must grow to love, without any complaints. I was taught that was what life is all about. You go to school, enter university, and major in a field you can (you hope) learn to love, then find an unpaid internship at a company; you work your ass off, eating McDonald's daily and living on a small allowance from your father while you climb the ladder.

While on this path, I had utterly lost motivation. I was internally conflicted; I couldn't live with myself knowing I am like everyone else, a robot designed to perform the task at hand. I couldn't accept such a philosophy or the lifestyle that came with it. I felt there must be something bigger out there for me. I didn't believe this was what God had planned for me. It was impossible! I had gone through enough hardship and monotony in Saudi Arabia to last a lifetime. I deserved to be happy. I would not settle for less. I had enough ambition to lead an entire nation.

I didn't realize that what I was missing was guidance. No one discovered my talents and guided me to take the right steps of practice to become the best I could be in a particular field, be it acting, singing, dancing, writing. I was on my own, with nothing but a dream and ambition. Perhaps these would be enough to keep me going.

In my next year at university, I took some acting workshops at night. It was exhausting after a long day at university in the cold winter, taking one bus to another, then catching the metro to go all the way up to Laval, then the bus again to get home, where I also had to make dinner. I wasn't accustomed to the workload—chores, schoolwork, and a part-time job so I could make extra pocket money to live more comfortably. After all, I was an adult; I had to work and make my own money, rather than waiting for Daddy to transfer funds after much begging and complaints. I became impatient, hungry for success; textbooks could not keep me still and steady. I couldn't keep it all in balance; my grades suffered to the point where I was suspended from University, and I quit my acting workshop. I had to get out there, grab a bite of life, and seize the moment. The Aries that I am, I was on fire and motivated to succeed.

With nothing left to hold me in Montreal, Saudi Arabia was calling again. I would work there for seven years in the fields of advertising and branding. I was making a very decent salary and other personal gains from a few deals here and there—enough to feel content for a while. My bank balance exceeded my expectations—especially when you consider that by the time I left Canada there was only $2.00 in my account in Desjardins.

However, the childhood dream of becoming an actor still lived inside of me and wouldn't die. I tried to find acting workshops or agents in Saudi Arabia; but unsurprisingly, a country banned that had cinemas was not the right place to become an actor, or even learn the basics of the craft. I felt this dream was unattainable, impossible. Perhaps acting was not my destiny after all. If it had been, then I would have started from a young age, like Britney Spears, Justin Timberlake, and Christina Aguilera (who all started in *The New Mickey Mouse Club*), or like Leonardo DiCaprio or Drew Barrymore, who were film stars before they even passed puberty. Acting was their specialty; it was all they'd ever known. Their parents, of course, had supported them every step of the way in their quests to be the best they could be in the entertainment industry. I believe the culture and community in which they grew up—that is, the United States, and particularly southern California—supported such various fields of arts and it was also a land of opportunities where different advanced fields of study existed, such as archeology, creative writing, instrumental performance, acting, choreography, and much more. The world they lived in was more advanced than my world, and the generations they came from were aware and enlightened.

My grandparents had fled from the war in Palestine in 1948, trekking to Lebanon in a pickup truck to save their lives and the lives of their children. They lived in unfortunate circumstances, where putting food on the table was more important than singing or dancing; and they surely did not want their children and grandchildren to have to face such horrifying circumstances in their lives. Empathizing with your elders—understanding why they do what they do—is very important to understanding both your past and your future. Knowing the sacrifices they needed to make will give you a fuller perspective on what you must do to reach your goal.

I was working as marketing director for a holding company of a billionaire Saudi family who owned amusement parks across the Middle East and India; one morning I received an email that the founder had decided to spend my marketing budget without my approval on a marketing plan that I had not devised. I realized that I could not just sit quietly and collect my salary at the end of the month in a place where my work was not appreciated or taken into consideration, a place where I had sacrificed my entire lifestyle for my career. I had reached my limit; I could no longer bear the ignorance and unawareness of these people. I knew I was much better than this. I was unhappy with my work; there was a calling that I had felt since I was a child that I kept suppressing, perhaps from fear of failure—or perhaps I was just in a rut. I knew that I deserved to be happy. I could decide to stop the pain and live however I wished, do whatever I wanted to do, by shutting out all the voices around me and listening more carefully to the voice within.

Hollywood was calling! Could it be possible that California—the land of Mickey Mouse, Marilyn Monroe, and Batman—was calling *moi*? *C'est pas possible!* I started to feel a sense of peace and happiness, slowly but surely. This was all I had ever wanted. I did my research on rent, cost of living, and airline fares; when I added up the numbers, I realized that I would be able to support myself for one year. One year, to see where the waves might lead me.

I had no intention to tell any professional acquaintances about my decision. I was serious about shutting out the voices from my surroundings that I did not wish to hear. I was focused and I made up my mind! In one month's time, I would leave for Los Angeles and no one could stop me.

That night, I went home and told my parents about my decision. They didn't seem to care; they were accustomed to me traveling around the world and believe that I would be back. They didn't expect I would actually go to live in California. I didn't sink in until they finally saw that I had resigned from the company, packed my four suitcases, lined them up near my bedroom door, and booked my ticket from RUH to LAX on Saudi Airlines.

My mother couldn't believe I would abandon a profitable career for such a sudden drastic change. My father seemed indifferent, but I could tell he saw something of himself in me; he, too, had fallen in love with Los Angeles. And at last he understood what I was going through, trying to find my path in life. We all did not prefer to live in Saudi Arabia, but it had given us more than what we could have expected, given where my father had come from. It's a long way from Palestine to Lebanon to Canada, then back to Saudi Arabia, where the entire family tree found stability—abundance, really, catering to the needs of their children where every child had an iPhone and maybe an iPad as well. Leaving this blessed country of wealth was too risky for them as they had a big responsibility. As for me, I was on my own. At my age, my father already had three children to feed and two brothers to take care of in Montreal. I was blessed to have the chance to find my true calling, my purpose in life, while I was still a young man, and follow my farfetched dream in the USA.

It was a sunny day with a temperature of 35 degrees Celsius in Burbank as I landed at Bob Hope Airport. I decided to begin my acting education immediately; in the baggage claim, I went up to an American woman waiting for her suitcases and asked her: "Who is Bob Hope, anyway?"

She was very obliging. She didn't know much about his history, but she knew he was an English-born American comedian and actor who had appeared in feature films and TV shows, and was the first comedian to entertain active service American military personnel. I later learned he had made fifty-seven tours for the USO between 1941 and 1991, and in recognition for his service was declared an honorary veteran of the United States Armed Forces in 1997 by an act of the US Congress.

I was proud to be at the center of the entertainment world, and to start learning about the early days of Hollywood entertainment. Let the journey begin!

Driving on Bob Hope Street in my Mustang convertible, I felt the hot breeze hitting my face as I gazed at the palm trees of California. Of course, we have palm trees in Saudi Arabia, too—but they simply seemed prettier in LA. Well, it is California, after all!

I felt refreshed by the sight of beautiful houses nearby each other without any surrounding walls. People were out on their bikes and rollerblades, full of life, living to the fullest. I could taste freedom as I drove in the beautiful hot city of Burbank down to Hollywood where I finally arrived at the street of dreams—Hollywood Boulevard.

The happiness with which I was overflowing was indescribable and overwhelming. I continued down to Sunset Boulevard, right to West Hollywood, and finally down to Beverly Hills. Rodeo Drive and the Beverly Hills Hotel were just two of the landmarks that sparked my attention; I had seen these landmarks in movies on the big screens.

It felt divine just to be in the homeplace of celebrities and actors, the home of Lisa Vanderpump and Charlie Sheen. I had never smiled so much as I did during that three-hour drive. People must have been staring at me, wondering why the hell I am smiling like Happy Gilmore. They wouldn't understand, and I didn't expect them to. I didn't care about anything except being present and taking in all that is present. It felt like being high on ecstasy—not that I would know.

After my little drive, I found my way back to Burbank with the help of the GPS in my iPhone, to the apartment I had rented on Riverside Drive. It was a new experience, as I had never rented my own place before. I learned about all the paperwork and insurance it entailed— opening an account with Burbank Water and Electricity and paying an initial deposit against so-called "possible damages." All this was new and somewhat exhausting. But when I finally got my keys and went to my one-bedroom apartment overlooking the hills of the back side of the Hollywood sign, looking out on the beautiful scenery, I felt a moment of serenity. I was finally here on my own, in my own place, following my own dream. I could finally be an actor, find true love, have a normal life, be free. Los Angeles was heaven on Earth. I was advised to drive to Target to buy some kitchenware and home supplies, and then to IKEA for some affordable furniture—starting with a bed to sleep on.

As I was driving on the clean road, I passed by one of the leading

TV and film production studios in the world, which came as a surprise. Gigantic billboards for popular shows such as *Two and a Half Men* and *The Ellen Show* decorated the fence surrounding none other than Warner Bros. I just parked my car across the street and stared at the entire structure standing only a few meters way. I literally was the only person staring, and I was filled with excitement. Could it be that I was the only one who is excited about seeing Warner Bros.? I didn't want to look like a tourist, so I continued to Target, knowing I'd be passing by this major studio every day, a landmark which had been in our lives since Day One.

The palm trees swayed as the sun shone down on the pavement, bringing out the details of the city. A beautiful breeze gusting against the skin quickens your appreciation of the green and the blue colors of the landscape. From the hills to the steepest valleys, this breeze pushes its way through, not leaving a fragment of your old thinking, bringing your full mind into momentum. A multicultural city bringing life to multiple forms of people from the hills to the valleys, from the rich to the poor, from sunrise to sunset; all is beautifully set.

Los Angeles is a paradise of good weather and a mecca for entertainers. But do not be fooled: it is where raw material is born, too, a real place with real splendor; it does not disguise itself, it does not exaggerate its image. What you see is real. Only in LA.

I came to Los Angeles on a mission: to engage the interest of leading producers, actors, and directors to produce my movie *Culture Clash*, for which I only had a treatment. I knew nearly nothing of filmmaking, but I had the motivation to get the ball rolling—and, just as importantly, I had a subscription to IMDb Pro, which gave me access to the contact information for Hollywood production companies and agencies. The story for *Culture Clash* was based on the book I had been writing for ten years, about a young man who moves to Saudi Arabia, the most suppressive Islamic nation in the world, as he fights to exist in the country and live a normal life. I knew I wanted Goldie Hawn to play the role of the mother in the film, as she looks similar to my mother with her long blonde hair. I was eager to contact her agent at CAA and pique her interest about filming this true story.

Casting Goldie Hawn in this film seemed right, as the world missed her on the big screen. From my marketing background, as per the focus group I conducted, viewers in their late twenties who lived most of the 1990s have missed Goldie.

When I got in touch with CAA, I told them I was the assistant to a prince of Saudi Arabia and we had a movie we wished to present to Goldie Hawn at once. I was passed over directly to her agent Fred. I told him that we had a treatment to present to Goldie, and that attaching her name to *Culture Clash* would help us raise funds.

The first words out of Fred's mouth were, "How much money have you already raised?"

"Nothing, at the moment," I admitted.

He replied that once we had financing in place, he would assist in getting me whoever I wanted. That is how Hollywood works. Finally, I understood that money was power and all I had to do was raise the funds to get my Goldie Hawn.

I started emailing and messaging numerous people in the industry, sending the treatment of the film, along with my headshot and beginner résumé, to acting agents. I received many replies of regrets. Only one so-called talent agent-slash-casting director decided to meet me. I only wish I wasn't filled with such excitement that I couldn't hit my brakes. This alleged agent called me to say that he was exceedingly interested, and that it was very important for me to build my reel. He had worked for the National Geographic Channel, he claimed, and had the connections to help get me on the channel as a paid host.

It was indeed thrilling— especially for someone who knew nothing of Hollywood scams. I met with the old man, who persuaded me to pay $800 to create a reel where I'd host a PSA. I didn't understand why I would pay to host someone's infomercial; he said it was to have some material for my reel. It was a standard arrangement, he said: aspiring actors would do two shows for them, then an editor would compile the clips (with some of their past work, if they had any) and create a reel for agents. I paid my initial deposit to the young Hollister-looking boy working in the agent's office, and we went to the Veteran's Hospital to shoot the PSAs. It was a great experience to get back to performing and learn the basics on the job and get my feet wet in the industry.

As time passed, I forgot about the PSAs; I never saw the footage, and moreover I had to sign a non-release contract saying that I couldn't use these clips online; the rights, I was told, belonged to some charity that turned out to be non-existent. It was only after two months that the office boy took pity on me and explained the workings of this fraud that targeted innocent people, novices in the industry in Hollywood.

This young man—just twenty-five years old—had also wanted to live the Hollywood dream ,and felt he was closer to success than ever by working with this con artist who sold hope to young boys and girls. Soon after telling me the truth, he quit his job and apologized to me in person, even visiting me in Burbank. I guess good-hearted Americans do exist! Nevertheless, I had not come to Hollywood to take an old man to court over a $400 deposit. Instead, I focused on my own work.

I decided to enroll in a few acting schools and studios to build my skills and sharpen my acting knowledge. The young man told me about the best studio in Los Angeles, Howard Fine Studios. Mr. Fine is one of the leading acting coaches for celebrities, having worked with Salma Hayek, Leonardo DiCaprio, Ryan Gosling, and many more. His work has been written about in the *New York Times* and in his own book, *Fine On Acting*, which I had to purchase upon my enrollment. I was given an appointment to do an audit on his class; I would watch how the acting instructor taught his class and have the opportunity to learn about the curriculum and about his style of working with the students.

I sat in this grand theatre among the students, waiting for the great man to appear. At last Mr. Fine swept into the room, followed by grand applause. I felt utter joy just to be in the same room with Howard Fine and in the actual theatre where I would finally learn some acting.

Mr. Fine would lay out the rules for each acting exercise, then sit in the back and call out a play title. A group of students would prepare the props, lay out the stage, and get into place; everyone would help and assist the assigned lead actors. The collaboration and teamwork among them was fascinating. I already felt insecure about simply presenting myself on stage, let alone helping out among twenty people out there.

An assistant called for silence as he saw the cue from the lead actors. The play began. I was enraptured. It was magical to see these students get into their costumes and characters and memorize every line. I was touched and amazed. I wanted to be them. I wanted to be a Howard Fine student.

When the play ended, Mr. Fine mounted the stage, where a chair would be positioned for him, and start his interrogation and commentaries. The first thing he asked each lead actor was: how did they feel? Then he would comment on each performance, imparting golden lessons in acting. It was so informative that I couldn't keep up as I took notes; every single thing he said was more valuable than the thing before.

Suddenly, my phone alarm rang. I was sure I'd had it on silent—but the alarm still rang aloud.

Mr. Fine looked around the room. "Whose phone is ringing?" he asked.

Embarrassed, I replied that it was my alarm.

"Exit now," he said.

I was heartbroken and mortified. I took my bag and passed by twenty-something students on my way up the stairs to exit the theatre.

When you want something really badly, obstacles will present themselves and test you. I came from 10,000 miles away for this; I wanted to act more than anything—or at least have a glimpse of the student experience. But even that may had been denied me. I was on the verge of tears. Something was ripped from my heart and lost forever.

After a while, I pulled myself together. I would deal with this constructively. "I'll be back, Mr. Howard Fine," I said to myself. "I am not quitting just yet; I certainly didn't come a long way from the middle of nowhere to end it here and now." I called the school again and booked another appointment for an audit. I would repeat the three-hour class again the next week, if that's what it took. Done!

This accomplished, I went to a bistro on Melrose. A waiter showed me to my table. The customer service in America is quite different than anywhere else in the world; for the Americans, customer does come first. I had scarcely sat down before the waiter was pouring me water, asking me if I was visiting or living in LA—chatting with me as if we were good friends. I wondered if he aiming for a big tip or if he was just a really nice guy.

We talked about the entertainment industry. He, too, was an actor, working part-time at the restaurant; in fact, we studied at Howard Fine Studios. This gave me a sense of relief, knowing that Howard Fine was an legitimate choice in this city of a thousand scams.

The waiter also worked as a bartender at a West Hollywood club on the weekends. Obviously he kept busy every hour. I realized that Americans have one thing in common; they are all hardworking and disciplined. Laziness is not in their vocabulary. They are young, and at the end of the day, they have to pay the bills, put food on the table, and make a living. I felt a wave of gratitude for how I had been blessed, given my hardships in the Kingdom.

No one has it easy in this life. We all have something going on, wherever we are. If you are in a free country, you barely have time for some fun because you work hard every day. If you are in a suppressed nation, you may live more comfortably—you can fill your gas tank for $20 at the most, for instance—because cost of living is cheap. Still others live in the most underdeveloped countries, where they can barely satisfy their basic needs; and yet they are among the happiest people on Earth. No matter where you are, you become accustomed to the lifestyle and take responsibility for the choices you make, based on your capabilities. You take the ride just like everyone else.

I believe we are all blessed in different ways. It is only selfish to say that one is blessed more than the other. Even Los Angeles, lovely as it is, is not perfect. It isn't the friendliest city in the world; everybody wants something, or wants to latch on to something or someone bigger than themselves. There were days where I felt like the loneliest person in the world. At least in Saudi Arabia, I'd had my best friends, my family, my colleagues and my work. In today's digital mobile ecosystem, it is becoming harder to make new friends, to trust people, and finally to fall in love.

Love exists, of course, but we see more and more of convenient relationships—especially in Los Angeles, where materialism and superficiality have taken over the souls of people. So many wish to simply fill the emptiness they feel, mistaking love for infatuation or lust. It is a city of beauties rather than angels.

I settled into a routine. I would attend my class at Howard Fine Studio in the morning, have my lunch on Sunset Boulevard, and maybe have a date or meet an acquaintance, and finally go to the gym for an hour. That is what the full day of a Canadian citizen who has no green card and is not eligible to work looks like. I would go home at 5:00 PM and switch on Netflix, which we didn't have back in Saudi Arabia. You can try it there, and you'll get a screen stating that it is not available in your region. My father once contacted Netflix with a proposal to purchase full regional exclusivity, but they replied that they were not interested in the Middle East at this time. Given the GDP per capita in Saudi Arabia of $5,000, and in Qatar $7,000, given the gap in content, and especially given that there are no movie theatres in Saudi Arabia, Netflix would profit greatly from the 17,000,000 middle- and upper-class households with access to Internet. Perhaps they have done a proper market visibility study—ah, but that is another business book to write.

I would wander from room to room in my small apartment, maybe drink a glass of wine, and boredom would start to kick in. I could not escape it in Saudi Arabia; I could not escape it in Canada, when I was at university. Now I was in the middle of the land of movies, in the same neighborhood as Warner Bros. Studios, and studying acting, and I was bored. I would ask myself: *What is wrong with me? Do I blame myself, or the country?*

Every other weekend, I would go out clubbing or stop at a bar to have a few drinks, and I realized that people from Los Angeles will not talk to you or introduce themselves; they certainly won't buy a round of drinks. It is always the New Yorkers who would engage me in an intelligent and friendly conversation. However, Americans in general are social and full of zest. Perhaps it was just my nervous energy, backed with negative thoughts, that made me rush to judgement about people and places—especially when I had only been there for three months. All I knew is that it was much better than where I had been. Period!

Every day, I woke up proud of my choice to leave everything I thought I had, to take on California—a dream I had since I was six years old.

I met a wise man at a bar one day. He was in his fifties, originally from New York, not from Los Angeles. He was asking me about my life and what brought me to Los Angeles. He took the last sip of his beer, looked me in the eyes, and said, "I think for you to come here all alone is the bravest thing and riskiest thing at the same time. And when the risks are higher, then so are the profits. You should be proud of yourself every day, settling in in such a short period of time like that. Pat yourself on the back right now and tell yourself, 'Good job!'"

I had never thought of myself that way. I was always pushing myself to go harder and faster, to reach the unattainable. However, I should be gentler to myself, letting my body and mental state start working toward what I want with peace of mind, trusting that everything will be OK, that I will make it no matter what. America is a country that rewards hard workers. I was also trying to ramp up from a slower and easier lifestyle to a faster and hardworking disciplined lifestyle, breaking old patterns and adapting to new habits.

In the meantime, I had met a few leading entertainment industry people and learned everything I could about the business. I learned how the film industry works and what producing a movie entails. I did my research about filmmaking; the job of a producer piqued my interest, as I fell in love with this particular field of work more and more. I visited

Barnes and Noble for related books and met industry players for dinner or drinks, reading studying, and listening attentively to every word. I loved the entire life cycle of a movie—how it starts from a script, lands on the desks of distributors, and finally lights up the big screen. I was amazed. I had found my true calling, the thing that makes me happy. I found the love of my life that I thought I would never meet. I feel in love with being a producer.

I've always known I was a storyteller. And that is the role of a producer. He's the man behind the big stories, putting every important element together to create a film. And the prospect of sharing in the profits of a major film—the "back end," in industry jargon—was very tempting. According to the Motion Picture Association of American, studios in the USA produce approximately 455 feature films a year with budgets of $1 million or higher. (Student films and lower-budget projects are not included in their accounting.) This puts the United States in the number three spot for film production, behind China with 638 films annually, and India with a massive 1,605.

However, the US and Canada rank as the top countries for ticket sales, with a gross box office total of $10.9 billion annually, followed by China at $3.54 billion. India is ranked sixth in the world.

Many factors play into the success of a movie. Even though major US-based studios such as Universal, Warner Bros., and Lionsgate are responsible for the top grossing box office movies worldwide, but there is a whole ecosystem of talent operating outside of that system. I was surrounded with waiters who were actors, students who were directors and cinematographers, and businessmen who were producers. I had to start somewhere, to find a way to show my talents and demonstrate my determination. The answer was affordable, realistic, and eminently possible—I would produce ten-minute short films.

On Saturday morning, I was out walking in Burbank. The sun was shining; people were out on St. Fernando Street in Burbank. My spirit was elevated, and a feeling of contentment came over me. As I walked, along Olive Street, a rush of story ideas for short movies flooded my mind. I guess it was the magic of Los Angeles. I rushed back home to my laptop and started writing. I knew almost nothing about how to write a script, but I had a great idea for a short comedy, which would be my first film.

Not long after. I met a young, passionate, good-looking gentleman called Alexander at Howard Fine Studios. We had clicked instantly after exchanging opinions about the Arab brand image worldwide and how it has been distorted in the media. On an impulse, I reached into my backpack and presented him with the short script I'd been working on. As he read the script, I was filled with anxiety; then his beautiful white smile filled the room with joy and positivity. He looked at me and said, "You complete my vision, Mr. Nathen."

Alexander agreed to fund, produce, and act in my project as his first experimental short film. I spent the next three weeks securing a director, casting actors, finding locations, and hiring a small crew— sound guy, cinematographer, and camera operator—to shoot the short, which was now entitled *Ahmed and Howard*. It's available to view now on YouTube and Indieflix. The film is about two young men, an Israeli and a Palestinian, divided by history and brought together at a grocery store to solve the Middle East crisis, one hummus at a time. The story played to my strengths—courting controversy and reenacting reality by telling the truth of what people really talk about every day.

Because I *wanted Ahmed and Howard* to showcase all my talents, I included a musical twist at the end (we live in the era of *Glee,* after all). The short could also serve as part of my reel. I wish I had known the filmmaking business before I invested with the con artist who claimed he could make me a star on the National Geographic Channel as a leading Arab-looking host. That $400 could have gone toward funding another short movie; but we live and learn. I kept a positive attitude during the making of the film, and learned the aspects of producing, acting, and dancing, as well as being assistant director.

I was utterly satisfied, and enjoyed every second of being on set with the crew and cast. The experience left me more convinced than ever that this is what I wanted to do for the rest of my life—tell stories. It is sad that I've loved acting since I was born, but my father failed to enroll me in a fine arts program; he had no respect for this field. and thought it was dirty. But what's past is past. My only choice now, in the present moment, was to ride the waves and become self-taught. The most successful entrepreneurs and artists were self-taught; life is the biggest school.

After making *Ahmed and Howard* I produced three more short films in a one-month period of one month. I was on fire. I was the heat. I couldn't stop. I couldn't live one minute away from the love of my life; I'd rather be in love with my work than go through heartbreaks and drama. In this career, I was the one at the steering wheel. In relationships, sometimes love takes you over and you can't control the course of your emotions. Anyway, I never imagined myself married with kids: who would love a man whose blood was contaminated? For me, love was farfetched and unattainable. But I came to a place of acceptance, and I grew to love myself and filmmaking even more.

Los Angeles had given me a purpose in life—a reason to wake up every day and work hard, fueled with passion and determination to succeed in the film industry. I realized how Hollywood always portrayed Arabs as terrorists or side characters, never placing us at the center of the story. My goal was to produce, write, and maybe even act in my own feature films, produced in Hollywood, promoting Arab stories and talents.

One of my inspirations, funnily enough, was Tyler Perry, who paved the way in our twenty-first century for African-American artists to promote their own type of comedy and drama. Arabs also have their own sense of humor, family ties and lies, culture, and traditions. We, too, deserved representation—and the results, if executed right, could very well be exceptional. Someone had to lead the way for Hollywood Arab cinema, someone with the vision to target a market niche and work with distributors in the Middle East, India, and China—which is the fastest growing film industry in the world, with cinemas opening with every breath we take. I finally envisioned what I wanted to be. I always knew the *kind* of man I wanted to become, but never found my purpose that would lead me to become him. Now I had.

Los Angeles was place where I found the inspiration and experience I needed to explore the talent hidden deep within my heart.

It was a land of creativity and vast diversification of art. I finally understood why people all over the world would say America was the land of dreams—although perhaps it would be more accurate to call it a land of inspiration. The USA may not offer your dreams to you on a silver platter, but it will guide you and offer you the tools to achieve them. If you have persistence, patience, and perseverance, you can definitely reach your goals, whether you're building innovative technology in Silicon Valley or acting in Hollywood.

After six months in Los Angeles, I had not won the lottery of either love or a green card. My time was up in the city of beauties. I could either relocate to Vancouver, which had strong Hollywood connections, or make a move to Dubai. The latter seemed like the best option to open my dream film production company. Dubai is an attractive film location; major Hollywood films, including installments in the *Mission: Impossible* and *Fast and the Furious* franchises, have been made there in recent years, and I saw an opportunity to position myself among other independent filmmakers building a bridge between Dubai and Hollywood. I could raise funds from investors in the oil countries to produce quality films in Hollywood, working with A-list actors and directors. I found a business strategy that was realistic and unique.

During my last month in Los Angeles, knowing I did not have enough time, I started brainstorming with creative screenplay writers on different genres of films with Middle Eastern themes, dreaming up an entire slate of movies available for funding—including a feature film extension of *Ahmed and Howard.*

I immersed myself in the creative process, engaging writers to write one treatment after the other until we had a satisfactory roster, and brought in script doctors with more than twenty years of experience in the entertainment field to polish the work.

When all was said and done, I had five feature film proposals, complete with treatments and scripts, to show to potential investors. I learned and mastered the art of selling and pitching films to buyers; my background in marketing and branding gave me insight into exactly how to promote the company. I incorporated a new business, Mazri Pictures, and was all set for Dubai—the country I had dreamt of from the big blue couch in Riyadh.

Dubai had it all—luxury, a western lifestyle, stunning film venues, vivacious nightlife, and a thriving tourism industry that drew visitors from across the globe, along with tolerant religious beliefs, respect for foreign cultures and faiths, and civil liberties that would be unthinkable to its neighboring countries. The move would also bring me closer to my parents, who I missed terribly. They were all I had, the only people who really accepted my mistakes, loved my insecurities, and believed in me. I had love for filmmaking and my parents. My heart had no more space for more love.

Love my parents though I did, I was anxious about returning to the Middle East. I had not spoken to my father in months. I assumed he resented me for being away, and I knew he disapproved of what he considered my sinful lifestyle. I understood where he came from, how he was raised; but above all I knew he loved me to death. Another religious Arab father would have kicked his son out of the house a long time ago for less than what I'd done. As a mature young man, I knew how to win his heart. I would empathize with him, listen as he spoke about what mattered to him.

I finally gave him a call to tell him the good news: that I was coming back to the Middle East, and had found my true calling in life. He started to open up to me, which I took as a good sign. He knew I would be back, and that gave him some satisfaction . He obviously needed me around to assist with his company, and simply for the sake of having his oldest son around; he is not getting any younger, after all.

All that my father ever wanted for me was to get married, have kids, and live a normal life; that's what he wished for his oldest son. I simply listened to his concerns with open ears. He wanted to be heard and respected, to feel a sense of validation. He is a father to five children, and the least thing he should expect is some degree of respect and agreement. In my early days, I was a rebel and he could smell it a hundred feet away. I antagonized him, building distance and misunderstanding. We came to resent each other, and at the same time blamed each other for our current situations—when in fact we only had ourselves to blame. He should blame himself for not being there for me more, for not mentoring me when he had the chance; I blame myself for failing to work through the culture clash on my own, for not realizing my father was doing his best, working day and night to provide for us.

We usually tend to blame others for our lives because we know that we don't have the strength to change our current situations; and we want to feed our righteous egos and cast ourselves as blameless. The power to change is in our hands only. I thank myself every day for traveling to Los Angeles and changing my life. My father never stood in the way of that, nor did Saudi culture. The only one standing in my way was me. I was my own enemy. I had to alter my perceptions and way of thinking about people, places, and life, by accepting my weaknesses and strengths to continually examining my expectations and perceptions.

What is the theme of Chapter 9?

There is no single path to success. Gandhi rose from India; Omar Sharif from Egypt; Celine Dion from Québec; William Shakespeare from England; Aristotle Onassis from Turkey. The sole driver of success is determination, the fire to succeed, and outweighing your indolence with hard work. This holds true no matter where you are in the world, even in the most oppressive country.

Fame is a branded illusion. Seek for a deeper purpose and the rest shall follow, whether you like it or not.

CHAPTER TEN

THE PREROGATIVE

Mazri's Law #10

You always have a choice. Your destiny is measured by how much you want it against how many bad choices you make against it. Choose what makes more sense, and the rest will fall into place—believe it or not!

On October 15, 2014, I was onboard a plane to Saudi Arabia once again. Sitting in economy class, I felt a sense of serenity and peace with myself. It didn't matter where I ended up living, whether in a developed or developing country. The place didn't bother me anymore. I was more in control of how my surroundings affected me, and I had more power over what people or stimuli would be permitted to enter my life. I was the master of my emotions, with a sense of self-confidence such as I had never felt, coming really from within. My serenity was contagious; the people I met could surely feel a sense of positivity and power emanating from me like an aura. People don't want to associate themselves with other weak and helpless people. As human beings, we desire to grow and evolve, to improve our standard of living, sharpen our skills, and reach the best of who we are. We always want better and strive to achieve nothing less. Finding a reason to live and a purpose in life makes everything else seem trivial. I could accept the insecurities of others; I felt above it all, for I had discovered my inner treasure—my passion and talent for entrepreneurship.

After a journey of almost twenty-two hours, I was excited to see my parents again. Since I'd departed for Los Angeles, my dear mother had not stopped crying. I remember that when I left, she had hidden behind the front door until I pulled away in the car, she couldn't bear the fact of my leaving. I could not wait to embrace her, to see the happiness in her face.

At last I could admit that I am a family guy at heart; the well-being of my parents ranks at the top of my priority list. It is only when you learn to love yourself that you can appreciate and love others. For years, I didn't realize how strong my love for my parents truly was, because I couldn't see past my narcissistic self. I was absorbed in my dreams of love, beauty, power, and happiness. But when we learn to give time to those who matter the most, rather than just ourselves— when we learn to give in order to receive—then we can truly achieve. Listening to one's calling and being introspective are the keys to self-fulfillment.

When I landed in Riyadh, the customs and airport advertising were noticeably improved. But that was about it: same old Riyadh. Our driver waited outside; we loaded up my luggage and took the King Fahad highway back home. Everything seemed strange to me, familiar and yet unfamiliar. I never thought I'd be back, but now I felt almost as if I had never been to this part of the world before. Yeah, right! I had endured more than the starving hyenas under Scar's rule in *The Lion King*. But all that was past. I was a new man, and I looked out at the Kingdom with a peaceful heart and a curious mind.

Back at home, I opened the gate while the driver took down the luggage. My younger brother Eddie opened the door of the house and greeted me with open arms. As I walked down the hallway toward the dining room, my mother emerged. She began to cry, looking broken. I hugged her tightly as she cried over my shoulders. I felt as if I had been lost, and now was found—a sensation which I never wanted to go through again. Life is too short to be apart, and you never know how long we have to walk above the ground together. It is not worth it to be divided.

I heard footsteps on the stairs, and turned around to see my father, wearing a smile that reached to his ears. This wasn't what I had expected; he hadn't spoken to me for months while I was in LA. Maybe it was his way of expressing his pain over the choices I had made. But now that I am back, he again felt a sense of peace; all he ever wanted was to keep me by his side, after all. He opened his arms and hugged me like never before, so tightly. What had I done to deserve such an embrace? Had I proved myself to him? Had I done something right? He whispered in my ear the answer to my question: "I love you, son!"

I cried over his shoulders. I knew that I was blessed to be loved. All my life I had been searching for validation and love, when all along it was right before my eyes. My second brother and sister watched the scene, looking at me as though I were a stranger. They were shy and polite. Maybe I should get away more often, if that's the respect I would get! My younger siblings admired me for following my dream, as no one in the family had ever done such a crazy thing. We all loved Los Angeles dearly, and had desired to work in the entertainment field since we were young brats. My sister loved to sing and write lyrics. Her writing was very poetic and filled with emotions. My brother also loved writing; he made rap music, and even had his own little recording studio in the basement when he lived in Montreal during his university years. We all knew were talented. but had never had the chance to follow our dreams. We were never taken seriously, as the Saudi education system did not value the arts, and our parents' generation never had the time.

Maybe we are a better version of what our parents were in life. I finally saw that I had the potential to inspire young people to pursue their dreams, to rise from the ashes by listening to your calling and not being afraid to seize it. This new insight came from watching my younger brother's behavior in how he would now talk to me and look up to me. He was somewhat impressed. I didn't know I had had such an impact on my siblings, or that my brothers had studied my every move.

My siblings were also struggling with life in the Kingdom. They too were learning to adapt to as they grew older; their minds expanded, and their needs changed. We all felt the need to live a normal life in this family, same as my mother and father.

That evening, as we had dinner, my father gave me the good news: we were *all* moving to Dubai, the whole family bound the land of abundance and extraordinary things, where my father had bought a six-room house. I screamed for joy. My mother was laughing, and my father was smiling. We finally did it—together!

Patience is indeed a virtue. After more than fourteen years living quietly, counting our blessings, dreaming and working as hard as everyone else, we finally had an exit strategy. We would still be near Saudi Arabia, but in a country where we could live normally—and most importantly, where we could be free.

Dubai has recently attracted world attention through many innovative large construction projects and sports events. The capital city's skyscrapers and high-rise buildings have become iconic, in particular the Burj Khalifa, the world's tallest building. In November 2013, Dubai won the right to host EXPO 2020. The beautiful Arabian Sea is the backdrop for complex of shopping malls and homes, the Beach by Meraas and Jumeirah Beach Residence; fine restaurants and top hotel chains, including Hilton, Marriott, and Ritz-Carlton, overlooked the glorious beach and the tourist hotspots. And soon, we would call this place home. Good things come to those who wait and work with a positive attitude.

Though I would shed no tears to leave Saudi Arabia, I had made my peace with the country. I had reached a state of knowing that happiness, success, and love come from within; it is not fulfilling to look for these golden secrets in a particular place, thing, or even another person. What Muslims have done all these centuries is keep true to their traditions and spirituality, maintaining their religious values. In North America, you don't always see this. Secularism has overshadowed religion. In the West, law seems more important than custom—with the end result that everyone wants to sue everyone else!

We Muslims have always believed that a pact with God was necessary for our well-being, survival, and success. Somehow in the west, we forget the higher power of creation that blesses us, that has saved us from many tragedies that might have befallen us otherwise. Religion does not define me. Rather, it empowers me with wisdom, with a belief in the unseen that keeps me true to my roots. Living in a suppressive environment allowed me to rebel, question, challenge, and doubt the world we live. I learned to think for myself, without peer pressure, and decide by my own choice and prerogative.

Suppression may be imposed by governing bodies, but they can't cage the human psyche. I still had my free will to think as I pleased, to decide for myself what I think is right or wrong. No one can ever take this away from me. Wherever I go, I will think the same; my thoughts will not change regardless of the country's beliefs or other people's ideas. I am what I say I think I am.

That said, a suppressive environment can cause a soul to crave for freedom, knowing no limits. And suppressed people may place themselves in danger as they push against their limitations. Suppression can create monsters in a given society. Governmental bodies must be more aware of the adverse effects of suppression on their people, especially the younger population. An oppressive nation hinders creativity, imagination, innovation, and vitality, leading to a closed-minded culture that causes depression and stress leading to chronic illnesses. Nations must comprehend the importance of the happiness index, and the economic benefits of happiness. Happiness results in a higher quality of well-being and lifestyle, increased GDP, higher productivity and employment, and stronger relationships between diverse groups of people from different religions, race, cultures, and income groups. These positive outcomes can't be achieved without freedom of will to which every human being is entitled. Governmental bodies must not punish human beings based on their freedom of will, but rather based on actions that may be harmful to others. Saudi Arabia is in constant battle to rein in the mutaween, the religious police who publicly harass people for disobeying the tenets of Wahhabism, even in ways that do no harm to anyone. These extremists wish to take away even the freedom of our own minds, to turn the Kingdom into a prison; that does not enhance the well-being of any human being.

We live in an individualized world, where self-expression is crucial to our well-being. We live our lives on Instagram, voluntarily exposing our daily lives to the world. Suppression may also occur online by limiting people's freedom of speech on Twitter and restricting access to the opinions of the people who were born with no chains and will die without them. Limiting someone's freedom to click, share, or post their own private thought is like entering their house without a warrant and dictating what they can say in their own home.

People are entitled to their opinions, the same way the government is entitled to its taxes or tariffs. If I had never lived in Saudi Arabia, I would never have come to terms with my purpose in life to fight oppression. I would never have understood that it was not a person, place, or thing that suppressed me, but rather that I suppressed my own thoughts and imagination. I was always free to control my reactions and attitudes to manifest what I desired in my life. Without Saudi Arabia, I would never have founded the new movement called *Arabiolosis*.

Today, I shall post #*TYKSA* ("Thank you. Kingdom of Saudi Arabia") for the man I am today; thank you for granting me the independent emotional intelligence and the control that will serve me in my life and business decisions. Suppression brings rise to unstoppable free will.

After my return to the Kingdom, I entered a Starbucks for men; as I was paying the cashier, I was suddenly poked from the back. It turned around to see my old best friend Roy: when we were kids, it was he who had once told me, "It doesn't suit you to be alone."

Roy was obviously taller now, darker, with a full Bin Laden beard—but he greeted me with a warm handshake. I sat with him for a while as he caught me up on his life. He was at the same advertising company he'd been at the last time I saw him; same country, never married, and same attitude, pretty much, for more than fourteen years now. It was shocking to see the same person at different times, who hasn't changed or isn't willing to improve.

Now, Roy had been following my exploits on Instagram and Facebook. He was curious about where I was in life. He was happy for me, and enthusiastically complimenting me with enthusiasm. But as he continued telling me his story, he was clearly stuck in his comfort zone, living a life of no surprises, a dull routine. The negative effects were plain; he had grown angry even toward the sweetest and most tolerant victim—his mother—over how he was unable to socialize with anyone.

He wanted to leave the country, but felt trapped; because he held a limited Lebanese passport, he would need a tourist visa and work permit anywhere he went. (Thank god for Trudeau!)

"What is it about this country," I asked, "that has trapped us— preventing us from living the same real life as the outside world?"

He offered a few excuses for settling into a life that didn't satisfy him: If only his father hadn't passed away, if only . . . if only . . . The list went on. He was clearly unhappy! I saw a broken bird behind the tough external surface.

I chose my words carefully, with consideration to his feelings. "Allow me to say with full condolences, that your father passed away when you were young to show you that life is short," I said. "Your father is now six feet under, and everything he owned is above ground. What has he taken away with him? Nothing!"

"That's true enough," Roy said.

"Life itself is what's valuable. Enjoy life! You have to take risks to see the profits. Great things come to those who seize them. Trust that you can do whatever you set your mind to." Thinking of Roy's Lebanese passport, I said, "I have seen hundreds of Lebanese men and women emigrate to Spain, London, and Canada with nothing. Now they have lives and children of their own."

"That sounds amazing," Roy answered. "But what should I do? How would it change things for me?" He seemed paralyzed. I empathized with him; I knew exactly how it felt when you faced a problem but had lost the knowledge of *How?*—how to solve it.

"You must have a lot of vacation days saved up," I said.

"Sure," said Roy. "Six weeks, at least."

"Then take one month off from work," I said. " A whole month, and go to Dubai for a month. Not for partying, though. Look for work. Talk to people. Network. Live in a free country, and learn how it feels again. Your soul needs an escape. Take some time away from this place to think clearly. You need to find out for yourself what you really want to be—what you want to do with this one short, valuable life of yours."

"I don't know, Nathen." Roy looked troubled "Maybe I'm not like you."

"What do you have to lose?" I asked. "Doesn't it bother you to see the whole world living on Facebook, uploading their pictures as they participate in this life—while you are simply the observer? Perhaps you are imprisoning your soul in this country because it's comfortable for you—but it isn't, really, is it? You're always traveling, spending money recklessly here and there when you could've invested it in something to bring you long-term happiness. But you are locked here because you choose to be. Your fear of the unknown has paralyzed you. You can't seize new opportunities and adventures because you're afraid to let go of what you already have, what you've been accustomed to for over a decade now."

I had not meant to speak so bluntly. I worried that Roy would be angry. But he only looked thoughtful. "You could be right, old friend," he said. "Maybe my best life is waiting for me."

"Well, brother, there's one way to find out," I said. "Learn to master introspection by balancing your thoughts, reasoning, and perception."

Roy smiled. "Those are some big words, Mr. Mazri."

"Go see what life may bring you in any country. That may be what it takes to show you that *you* are in the driver's seat," I said. "Your destiny will not change because you physically moved from one place to another. Your destiny is your fate—no matter when, where, or what."

"If I do go," said Roy, "what advice would you give me?"

"Be open to listening to what's around you—not to the negative thoughts inside, not to your chatterbox," I said. "Saudi Arabia made me the man I am today, turned a broken, angry bird into an eagle full of understanding and enlightenment. Set your mind to positivity, Roy. See the boundless opportunities. You can be the change you want to see— *now,* not tomorrow. You can do this."

"You inspire me," said Roy, then smiled. "But how did *you* become a man of such unexpected wisdom at a young age? You were the class clown? What is even your purpose?"

I looked away for a moment. I had visited this same Starbucks when I was young. I remembered being sixteen years old, gazing through the window, feeling this peculiar world was passing me by.

At last, I turned to Roy and replied, "Be introspective. Everything changes in the world around you. This influences your thoughts. So you must always make time to meet yourself within. Take a moment to be aware of your every thought and emotion—without consideration, without judgment—even if you are in the middle of the desert."

Roy interrupted. "But I ask again: What is *your* purpose, Nathen?"

But I continued: "You must examine your own thoughts and perceptions of yourself and others constantly if you desire to thrive and succeed with high self-esteem in the public eye. like any perfect Caucasian American human being out there in the world as so it seems because the bogus media is coming after every single one of us Arabs."

I leaned in close to Roy and said, "I am what I think, no matter where I am or how others perceive me!"

Roy became frustrated. "Are you going to answer my question? What is *your* purpose, Nathen?"

I looked away, watching the cars that drove by in the busy streets of modern Riyadh; then said, "TYKSA."

"TYKSA?" Roy said curiously. "What's that?"

Still looking out the window, I could see in the distance the beautiful Al Faisaliah Tower, designed by the architect, Norman Foster. "Thank you, Kingdom of Saudi Arabia."

"For what?"

I finally turned to Roy, looking into his eyes with a proud smile. "For being introspective. I think I'm a clairempath, Roy."

What is the theme of Chapter 10?

You will never discover yourself until you fight suppression.

Never allow a place, person, or thing stop you from living—thinking and feeling.